THE BATTLES OF
CORONEL AND
THE FALKLANDS

THE BATTLES OF
CORONEL AND THE FALKLANDS

BRITISH NAVAL CAMPAIGNS IN THE SOUTHERN HEMISPHERE 1914-1915

PHIL CARRADICE

FONTHILL

In memory of Robert Turnbull Carradice and
Jack Matheson Carradice—got there at last!

Fonthill Media Language Policy

Fonthill Media publishes in the international English language market. One language edition is published worldwide. As there are minor differences in spelling and presentation, especially with regard to American English and British English, a policy is necessary to define which form of English to use. The Fonthill Policy is to use the form of English native to the author. Phil Carradice was born and educated in Pembroke Dock and at Cardiff University, and now lives in the Vale of Glamorgan, therefore British English has been adopted in this publication.

Fonthill Media Limited
Fonthill Media LLC
www.fonthillmedia.com
office@fonthillmedia.com

First published in the United Kingdom
and the United States of America 2014

British Library Cataloguing in Publication Data:
A catalogue record for this book is available from the British Library

Copyright © Phil Carradice 2014

ISBN 978-1-78155-347-3

Typeset in 11pt on 13pt Sabon
Printed and bound by CPI Group (UK) Ltd, Croydon, CR0 4YY

Contents

Acknowledgements

Thanks are due to many people who have helped in the research and writing of this book:–

To begin with, my father and grandfather who first told me about the tragedy and glory of Coronel and the Falklands. Their interest—my grandfather having been an engineer officer in the RFA during the Great War, my father a life-long student of nautical matters—was passed onto me. I always said that one day I would write about the campaigns that so intrigued them. This is it. I only hope they would have approved.

The staff of Cardiff and Penarth Libraries who put up with my many mindless queries and questions.

Then Roger MacCallum, friend and ex-rugby playing compatriot, whose interest matched my own—and whose technical mastery and skill were essential components in the making of this volume.

Trudy, my wife. Without your support and understanding, this would still be little more than an idea. Thank you.

About the Author

Phil Carradice is a novelist, poet and historian who has written over forty books. Among the most recent are A Pembrokeshire Childhood and The Ships of Pembroke Dockyard, both for Amberley Publishing and Do Not Go Gentle, a novel about Dylan Thomas. For Fonthill he has recently written a biography of the writer Charles Dickens. He is a regular broadcaster on BBC radio and writes a weekly blog for BBC Wales History.

Introduction

The naval campaigns in the southern hemisphere during final months of 1914 and the early part of 1915 were the last sea battles to be fought without the intrusion of the modern technological marvels. In the early months of the First World War these technical marvels—weapons and machines like wireless telegraphy, aeroplanes and submarines—were still revolutionary and in an embryonic state. And so the battles of 1914 and 1915 in the southern seas were fought without them. Almost.

Aircraft were actually used during the destruction of the *Königsberg* even though it was the big guns of the British monitors that finally sank the raider. But apart from this one instance, the Battles of Coronel and the Falkland Islands were fought in almost the same way as the sea fights of Nelson a century before when two battle fleets drew up opposite each other and relied on accurate gunfire—or, at the very least, weight of gunfire—to win the day.

The ranges might have been longer, the shells and weapons more deadly and the means of propelling them more efficient, but the natural elements—things like wind, rain, snow and fog—were still a vital component in the success or failure of any fleet action.

Instant communication from the south seas to London or Berlin were still things of the future. It took hours, maybe even days, for messages to get back to base. Winston Churchill at the Admiralty, for example, did not hear about battle being joined outside Port Stanley until most of von Spee's Squadron had already been sent to the bottom of the ocean.

The naval war in the southern hemisphere was dominated by coal. Without coal the ships simply would not move and so admirals and captains from both sides plotted their campaigns around this vital commodity. It was easier for the British, of course, with their network of coaling stations, colonies and remote outposts but for both sides lack or excess of coal was perhaps the most important aspect of the war.

At the conclusion of the campaign, the German naval presence in the southern hemisphere was wiped out and, thereafter, the war at sea gradually came down to the stalemate in the North Sea. The big battle fleets came out only once, to meet at the tactically inconclusive Battle of Jutland.

From a strategic point of view Jutland was a British victory but the increasing German reliance on their U-Boat fleet, it can be argued, was as a result not just of Jutland but also of their lack of naval presence elsewhere in the world after the crushing defeat of Admiral von Spee at the Battle of the Falkland Islands.

The campaigns in the southern hemisphere in 1914 and 1915 touched all corners of the globe—the Pacific, Indian and Atlantic Oceans, the African and Indian coasts, the rugged and clenched southern fists of South America. From exotic south sea islands to remote Atlantic outcrops, German and British fleets saw them all.

It was a bloody and brutal war, one fought to the death with matchless courage on both sides. The heroism of the men, the terrible mistakes that cost them so dearly, this was a campaign of attrition where success or failure often hung in the balance right to the end.

To mis-quote Robert Falcon Scott's earlier words about his Polar companion Captain Oates, it was a war fought by 'truly gallant gentlemen.'

1

Hostilities Commence

A Prologue

It is November 1913, the night humid, hot and sultry. Vice Admiral Maximilian von Spee and his officers rise to their feet, the admiral to propose, and the officers to drink, a toast to King George V of England and Kaiser Wilhelm II of Germany. It is past midnight and the scene is the wardroom of von Spee's new armoured cruiser *Scharnhorst*, rocking gently in the swell of Hong Kong harbour.

Von Spee's guests in the wardroom are the officers of HMS *Monmouth*, their tour of duty in the Far East finally over. The English sailors are content, happy that they about to return to home waters. The meal finished, dancing with the invited ladies begins and the officers of both ships wander out to the quarter deck rail where they puff at their cigars and gaze out over the lights of the British colony. They are young men in love with life, with their ships and their careers. Their laughter and chatter echo around deck of the *Scharnhorst* and the glittering, exotic harbour.

Only the German admiral, von Spee, a man far sighted and experienced in the ways of the world, is pensive. He has been in command of this squadron for just over a month and is well aware of the pressures and tensions that are building back home in Germany. He knows that, sooner or later, there will be war. War against England.

Von Spee likes the English sailors, respects their judgement and their knowledge. But more than that, he fears them. If war does come, he thinks, they have the mightiest navy in the world. He knows what his task will be, here in the distant waters of the southern hemisphere, and he knows that he and all of the German East Asiatic Squadron are expendable. The admiral will do his duty. But he wonders how many of the young men he has entertained tonight, British and German alike, will survive the coming conflict. And he wonders how soon that conflict will be in coming. Insightful as he is, von Spee cannot possibly know that within twelve months the *Scharnhorst* and the *Monmouth* will meet again and that this time there will be no pleasant conversation, no toasts and most certainly no dancing.

Maximilian von Spee, commander of the German East Asiatic Squadron. A mercurial man and a tactical genius, long before war broke out he saw quite clearly what was coming and knew that he would be lucky to survive any conflict with the Royal Navy.

The armoured cruiser *Scharnhorst*, flagship of von Spee and a formidable ship of war. As with all German warships, her crew was well-trained and were expert at the all-important skill of marksmanship and gunnery.

H.M.S. MONMOUTH.

The British armoured cruiser *Monmouth*, a ship that was old and obsolete long before August 1914. She was the product of poor design, her lower gun ports virtually unworkable in a heavy sea. HMS *Monmouth* was one of ten armoured cruisers of her class, launched in 1901 and commissioned in 1903. In 1906 she was transferred to the China Station and remained there until she returned home in 1913 and was assigned to the reserve Third Fleet. When the War began the ship was recommissioned and assigned to the 5th Cruiser Squadron in the Central Atlantic to search for German commerce raiders and protect Allied shipping.

War

When war between Britain and Germany was declared on 4 August 1914, Britain—and specifically the Royal Navy—was in an unusually advantageous position. The previous month, in the middle of July, there had been a practice mobilisation of the Third—or Reserve—Fleet. It had been planned for several months and the fact that it coincided with the assassination of Archduke Franz Ferdinand in Sarajevo and the subsequent rise in tension in European capitals was mere chance. As far as the British were concerned, nobody expected war, whatever might be happening across the Channel. The Kaiser might be sabre rattling and making threats to Russia and France but nothing would come of them. It had all happened before and passed off peacefully enough.

This mobilisation was nothing unusual, either. For the 20,000 Reservists brought back to their ships, such calls to return to duty were to be expected, both from time-served men who had seen out the terms of their enlistment or those who were easing through their final years in the service and passing on their skills in the training establishments. It was part of the contract they had signed when they first joined the Royal Navy. And when the newspapers reported the gathering of the Reservists they did so with more than a degree of self-satisfaction:–

> Nearly 14,000 men of the Royal Fleet Reserves will today report themselves at the Naval Depots of Portsmouth, Chatham and Devonport. Every available officer and man will be withdrawn from the educational establishments—the gunnery, torpedo, navigation and signalling schools, and the War College—and almost the whole of our naval forces in home waters will be fully manned and placed—nominally at least—on a war footing.[1]

As part of the mobilisation there was also, on 18 July, a massive review of the First, Second and Third Fleets at Spithead, followed by exercises in the English Channel. Hundreds of Dreadnought and pre-Dreadnought battleships, cruisers and destroyers, not to mention thousands of sailors, were involved. The plan, then, was for the ships to return to their ports and for the Reservists and Instructors to head home or back to their training bases.

However, with the situation in Europe worsening by the hour, there were fears of a lightning attack on the British coast by units of the German fleet, and Prince Louis of Battenberg, the First Sea Lord, promptly cancelled the demobilisation. It was a decision reached by Prince Louis without any form of consultation but, when he heard the news Winston Churchill, First Lord of the Admiralty, quietly and immediately approved of the action.

On 18 July 1914 the Royal Navy held a huge Review, followed by Fleet manoeuvres, at Spithead—a lucky accident as it meant that most Reservists had been recalled and all ships were ready for action when war broke out.

Some men had already left their ships but these were promptly recalled and while, in many quarters, there was rejoicing at the prospect of finally giving the Kaiser the 'bloody nose' he richly deserved there were also very real fears about what might lie ahead:–

[*There was*] great enthusiasm as various contingents from the neighbouring towns arrived to entrain for Devonport, Plymouth and other naval depots—The enthusiastic crowd grew to such proportions that the station gates had to be closed and a posse of police was introduced to regulate the crowd—In the crowd there were many seriously visaged people and many who were moved to tears at the call for their husbands and sons.[2]

Despite the emotion, it meant that by the end of July the Royal Navy was on a clear war footing and the ships, suitably darkened and shrouded at night, were at their appropriate stations. Britain was protected and the whole population of the country basked in the knowledge that the Royal Navy was a bastion that would never be broached.

The Naval Race

For years the building of capital ships had been at the forefront of everyone's mind. Ever since the Kaiser had come to Britain for the great Naval Review held to celebrate Queen Victoria's Diamond Jubilee in 1897 he had been obsessed with building a fleet of battleships to match those of the Royal Navy.

Following the success of Admiral Von Tirpitz in getting the first Navy Bill through the Reichstag in 1898, the great 'Navy Race' of the early twentieth century swung into action. It saw both Britain and Germany building Dreadnoughts and battle cruisers at a rapid rate with Britain managing to keep her nose in front.

The German threat did not go away. A memorandum added to the German Navy Bill (subsequently an Act) of 1900 was clear that Germany had to have a fleet 'so strong that even for the strongest sea power, a war against it would involve such dangers as to imperil its position in the world.' For 'strongest sea power' read Britain.

And in Britain, public opinion was clear—there had to be a two-power standard. In other words, two British Dreadnoughts for every one German capital ship.

As Admiral Jacky Fisher once said, if Germany had a fleet within a few hours sailing of England, then the Royal Navy needed a fleet twice as strong to counter the threat. Public opinion was behind him. When, in 1909, news was released of Government plans to build just four new Dreadnoughts the following year, crowds thronged the streets in front of the Admiralty chanting 'We want eight and we won't wait.'

Left: The German Kaiser Wilhelm II, a man consumed by envy of the British Empire and, in particular, of the strength and power of the Royal Navy. Here he is in the uniform of an admiral in the *Kaiserliche Marine*.

Below: The Kaiser authorised huge expenditure to build the *Kaiserliche Marine*—the Imperial German Navy and in his ambition he found an ally in Grand Admiral Tirpitz. Following the Boxer rebellion in China and the Boer War, a second navy bill was passed on 14 June 1900. This approximately doubled the allocated number of ships to 38 battleships, 20 armoured cruisers, 38 light cruisers. Significantly, the bill set no overall cost limit for the building programme. This contemporary illustration shows the Kaiser on board *Deutschland*, reviewing the High Seas Fleet.

Grand Admiral Alfred von Tirpitz (1849–1930), the strength behind the throne. He was the man who, at the Kaiser's bidding, effectively created the German High Seas Fleet and set into motion the Naval Race that saw Britain and Germany building more and more Dreadnoughts every year. Expenditure for the navy was too great to be met from taxation: the Reichstag had limited powers to extend taxation without entering into negotiations with the constituent German states, and this was considered politically unviable. Instead, the bill was financed by massive loans. Tirpitz, in 1899 was already exploring the possibilities for extending the battleship total to 45, a target which rose to 48 by 1909. Tirpitz's ultimate goal was a fleet superior to that of Britain.

The public got its way. Winston Churchill, tongue pressed firmly into his cheek, later commented that the Admiralty wanted six new Dreadnoughts, economists offered four—and so they compromised on eight!

When, shortly before midnight on 4 August, the message 'Commence hostilities against Germany' was flashed to all Royal Navy ships, the Grand Fleet at Scapa Flow—just one of three major British battle groups—could boast 21 Dreadnoughts, 8 pre-Dreadnoughts, 4 battle cruisers and countless support craft. In contrast Germany's High Seas Fleet consisted of 13 Dreadnoughts, 16 pre-Dreadnoughts and 5 battle cruisers.

In the event of war, the German High Command and Admiralty had expected a close blockade of their coast, a situation that would be uncomfortable but which would enable their fleet to make lightning raids against the watching British vessels. Instead, after 4 August what was implemented was a distant blockade with the Straits of Dover in the south and the seas to the north of Scotland defended in strength by the Dover Patrol and the Grand Fleet respectively.

With regular cruiser, destroyer and battle cruiser sweeps across the North Sea, the waters off Britain's east coast had effectively become a British ocean, the tactic cleverly bottling up the High Seas Fleet in port. There it remained, always a threat but otherwise inactive, only once venturing out to give battle. Its actual impact on the course of the war was limited. The same could not be said of Germany's distant fleets and squadrons.

Raiders

In 1914 Britain possessed the greatest Empire the world had ever known. But it had one major weakness. As a small island nation the country depended on vital imports to survive—food, raw materials, manpower, even weapons—and all of it came into Britain by ship. Destroy those ships and the trading and coaling bases that supplied them, reasoned Grand Admiral Alfred von Tirpitz, Secretary of State for the German Navy, and you would go some way towards winning the war.

While Tirpitz, perhaps the leading pro-Dreadnought figure in Germany, would have liked to use capital ships to destroy British trade, he was realistic enough to see that such a plan was never going to work. If his Dreadnoughts were to be contained in port at Wilhelmshaven, then cruiser warfare would have to suffice. The raider concept was born.

From 1900 onwards the use of cruisers in waters far away from Germany was carefully thought out and large numbers of fast, efficient and heavily armed ships were built—in complete contrast to Britain where the mind set of naval planners and architects was focused solely on building bigger and better Dreadnoughts.

Those British armoured and protected cruisers that did roll off the stocks from dockyards like Chatham, Portsmouth, Rosyth and Pembroke Dock were virtually obsolete even before they were completed. They were hindered by slow speeds, limited armour and guns that were often mounted so low to the waterline that they were unusable in anything like a heavy sea.

In contrast German cruiser building in the ten years after 1900 was exemplary. Typical of the type were the *Scharnhorst* and *Gneisenau*, sister ships launched in 1907 and 1908. Although armed with 8.2 and 5.9 inch guns, these weapons were considerably more accurate and had a greater range than the larger calibres used on British cruisers of the time. They were also much faster than British armoured cruisers and were more than a match for almost anything below battle cruiser strength. Their high freeboard and heavy top gear, despite their appearance, did not make them poor sea boats. On the contrary, they were particularly stable and thus made good gun platforms.

Germany, therefore, had the ships to compete in foreign waters but what about the ports and bases to sustain them? Admiral Tirpitz himself was instrumental in founding the German cruiser base at Tsingtao on the coast of China, initially little more than a simple fishing community but soon transformed into a vibrant and bustling colony that proudly flew the German flag in the Far East. This was the base of the German East Asiatic Squadron, commanded by Admiral von Spee and made up of the armoured cruisers *Scharnhorst* and *Gneisenau* and the light cruisers *Nürnberg*, *Leipzig* and *Emden*.

Tsingtao might have been the nominal base of the German cruisers. However, such ships had to have the ability to roam far and near and in the years leading up to the outbreak of war German vessels were as likely to be found visiting

British cruiser design in the first ten or twelve years of the twentieth century was poor. Speed, armour and armament were totally inadequate. This shows the launch of the armoured cruiser *Defence* from Pembroke Dockyard in April 1907.

The *Gneisenau*, a typically effective and efficient German armoured cruiser built to operate independently, far from home, is shown here on a postcard from 1908.

The port of Tsingtao, Germany's toe hold in the Far East and, nominally at least, the home of the East Asiatic Squadron.

British bases like Hong Kong and Cape Town as they were moored in their own home port. The important thing was that they were at large in the southern hemisphere, not blockaded into ports where their only value was the threat that they might one day try to break out.

In the summer of 1914 Germany's Dreadnoughts were all based in the north but she still had several ships in and around the southern hemisphere. The *Karlsruhe* and *Dresden*, fast and modern light cruisers, were in the Caribbean but only a few day's fast steaming would, if necessary, bring them south to rendezvous with von Spee. *Dresden* had recently been relieved by the *Karlsruhe* and was supposedly heading back to Germany for a refit but the outbreak of war prevented that.

The *Königsberg*, nominally based at Dar-es-Salam, was somewhere in the Indian Ocean, her exact location unknown. A modern, fast light cruiser, she was a latent but potentially dangerous threat to British shipping in the Indian Ocean and off the African coast.

The battle cruiser *Goeben*, together with the modern light cruiser *Breslau,* were in the Mediterranean but a breakout through the Straits of Gibraltar into the South Atlantic was always a possibility that haunted British naval planners even after the two ships had run the gauntlet of waiting British forces and anchored off the Turkish city of Constantinople.

After August 1914, nearly forty passenger vessels of the Hamburg-Amerika and Norddeutscher Lines had been blockaded into ports in Germany and America. And that was just the tip of the iceberg. Several hundred liners and cargo vessels of various German lines were potentially available for conversion into armed merchant cruisers as soon as war began. Very few of the liners ever managed to get past patrolling British cruisers but five vessels, all fully converted into armed cruisers, did manage to run the blockade and within a few days of war breaking out were loose at sea. They added yet another threat to British shipping.

Armed merchant cruisers were hardly the most effective fighting vessels but both Britain and Germany used them widely in the early days of the war. Intended, initially, to fight ships of a similar nature and to engage in commerce raiding, many of the German ships had been fitted with gun platforms long before war broke out. They were, at best, a stop gap response and in a traditional line of battle combat they would, with their high freeboard and total lack of armour, be more of a hindrance than a help.

The German Plan

German war orders for von Spee and the East Asiatic Squadron were clearly mapped out—and so was their ultimate destiny:–

> Our ships abroad cannot count in wartime either on reinforcements or large quantities of supplies—The aim of cruiser warfare is to damage enemy trade; this must be effected by engaging equal or inferior enemy forces, if necessary.[3]

SMS *Dresden* passing through the Kiel Canal sometime between 1908 and the summer of 1909. This was shortly after she had been commissioned.

SMS *Dresden* in pre-war years, seen here in pristine condition at New York in 1909.

The German light cruiser *Dresden*, shown here in her final days, hiding in the fiords and creeks of Chile. The sister ship of the famed *Emden*, she was renowned as one of the fastest ships in the German Navy.

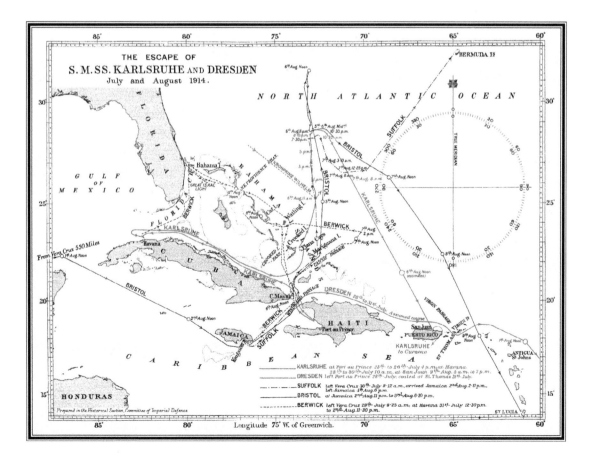

Nobody, certainly not Grand Admiral Tirpitz, could quite forget the hulking battleships of the High Seas Fleet, however, and there was another aim behind the concept of the raiders and the conduct of the cruiser war in the southern hemisphere:–

> The conduct of the naval war in home waters must be assisted by holding as many of the enemy's forces as possible in foreign waters.[4]

The eventual loss of the cruisers was taken for granted by the German Admiralty. Isolated and far from home they had neither the support services nor the network of repair bases and coaling stations that the British could call on whenever they were required. So they had always been considered something of a disposable asset.

But before they were hunted down and destroyed the cruisers were expected to inflict a heavy toll on British shipping. It would be a far from easy task.

The isolated port of Tsingtao, particularly once Japan entered the war on the side of the Allies at the end of August 1914, would quickly become as much a bottleneck for the East Asiatic Squadron as Wilhelmshaven had for the Dreadnoughts of the High Seas Fleet—as von Spee knew well enough. In times of war it would be almost unusable.

Therefore, he would have to become a rover, coaling his squadron from captured cargo vessels and meeting with furtive supply ships in hidden creeks or in safe neutral harbours. A list of suitable anchorages had long been available to the admiral and his cruiser captains and there were many German or friendly colliers in various parts of the Pacific and South Atlantic ready to pass over their cargoes—for a healthy fee, of course.

For von Spee, the advantages of being a 'free agent'—a modern day pirate—were many. He could foster and develop the element of surprise, no merchant skipper or Royal Navy captain knowing where he might turn up next. He could plunder his prizes for coal and food supplies, using the very things that the British valued so much, for his own ends. But there was also a very serious downside. Sitting on his flagship at Pagan Island in the South Pacific, waiting for the telegram informing him to begin hostilities, von Spee was acutely aware that damage to any one of his ships was liable to prove fatal. He had no repair facilities available to him and so he could not risk action against anything like a superior force.

Von Spee knew that his target would be merchantmen. To a man schooled in the traditions of the German Navy it was not, perhaps, the most palatable way to fight a war. But it was necessary and clearly the best way to hit at the vast might of the British Empire. Von Spee would fight this war in the only way known to him, with honour, courage and skill, but he could not help thinking that the months ahead would bring danger that could end only one way. Before that, however, von Spee had a decision to make—should he disperse his fleet and allow his captains to conduct individual raider campaigns or should he keep his ships together. By the time war was declared he had made up his mind. He would:

The raider *Emden*, perhaps the most famous German ship of the war, and her commander Captain Karl von Müller. The *Emden* fought a lone campaign, ranging across the Indian Ocean and confounding the Royal Navy for many months.

… keep the squadron together and disappear, cruising slowly amongst the distant and uninhabited islands, using up as little coal as possible, while his enemies wasted energy and weeks in searching for him.[5]

Only in that way, he decided, could he keep his ships safe—as safe as was possible anyway. And certainly by staying together he could cause considerable fear and disruption to the enemy convoy and supply routes. Only Captain Karl von Müller of the *Emden* disagreed.

Always a man of independent character, an idealist who was prepared to back his hunches with his actions, he saw no future in the fleet remaining together as one unit. They might well sail together and even fight together but von Müller knew they could also die together. And so he asked permission to wage a lone war. It was agreed and Müller sailed away to the west, both he and his admiral knowing that the chances of them meeting again were very slim.

On 12 August, just over a week after war was declared, the *Scharnhorst* and the rest of the East Asiatic Squadron slipped their moorings and disappeared into the wastes of the Pacific Ocean. The war in the southern hemisphere had begun.

2

Towards Disaster—British Dispositions at 4 August

At first glance it seemed as if Britain and her Allies had more than enough firepower to deal with any German threat in the southern seas. As well as the French Atlantic Fleet at Brest, by 4 August two British squadrons were patrolling the dangerous waters of the South Atlantic. Admiral Archibald Stoddart commanded the 5th Cruiser Squadron on what was known as the Southern Station while Admiral Christopher 'Kit' Craddock was with the 4th Cruiser Squadron in the West Indies. Both, or either of them, could head south, east or west at a moment's notice.

In addition there was Admiral Jerram at Hong Kong, his command consisting of four cruisers, a number of destroyers and the battleship *Triumph*. Admittedly the *Triumph* was an old pre-Dreadnought but her four ten inch guns would provide a considerable weight of broadside, should it ever be required.

East of Singapore lay the domain of the Australian Navy, a force that consisted of several cruisers and destroyers and the modern, powerful battle cruiser *Australia*. Equally as significant, with Japan declaring war on Germany, their up to date, well-equipped navy—a fighting force that, less than ten years before, had decimated the Russian fleet at the Battle of Tsushima—was also available to deal with the threat of the raiders.

As few trade routes went through the waters off East Africa, British forces in the western part of the Indian Ocean were somewhat limited. It was, planners felt, a backwater. The Cape Squadron under the command of Admiral Sir George Fowler King-Hall therefore consisted of just three light cruisers—the *Pegasus*, *Astraea* and *Hyacinth*, all of them out of date and first commissioned well before 1900—and none of them, if it ever came to battle, any possible match for the lurking *Königsberg*.

In the eastern Indian Ocean was Admiral Peirse. His force consisted of two light cruisers, a few sloops and the old battleship Swiftsure. Before the *Swiftsure* was taken away from him to help protect British interests along the Suez Canal, Peirse's force was certainly stronger than that of King-Hall although, as with so many of the British dispositions at this time, it was not as powerful as might first appear.

HMS *Hyacinth*, one of three old and out-dated cruisers charged with defending the western part of the Indian Ocean.

In fact, the whole situation was dangerously deceptive. The Allied forces were widely spread and consisted, in the main, of ships that were not only old and slow but which suffered from the poor design that haunted British cruisers in the early twentieth century. They were inadequately armed and even if they had the speed to catch the raiders, their fire power and limited armour plating would inevitably lead them only to disaster.

A decision had been taken to leave control of the Mediterranean to the French but national pride insisted that a British force be maintained there. After all, this inland sea had once been the premier posting for all British captains, men like Jacky Fisher being proud of their connections with Malta and the other ports that were synonymous with the British Empire. Consequently, a fleet of four battle cruisers, several armoured cruisers and numerous other ships was stationed in the Mediterranean, vessels that could and should have been employed elsewhere. Kit Craddock, in particular, would have welcomed then eagerly into his squadron.

Meanwhile von Spee, with his decision to keep the fleet together, had established what might be termed 'the inside lines of communication.' And hunting for him in the vast emptiness of the south and eastern Pacific was a thankless task.

Even Churchill, then serving as First Lord of the Admiralty, finally began to realise the grave inadequacy of the situation and some awareness of the enormity of the task facing his commanders in the southern hemisphere at last appeared to strike. Within a few weeks of the outbreak of war the 6th Cruiser Squadron was dispersed and part of it removed from the Grand Fleet. The idea was to

Admiral Christopher Kit Craddock, beloved of his men but no match for the wily von Spee—particularly when he was hampered with inadequate ships and an Admiralty that simply did not understand his difficulties.

send more ships south to help Kit Craddock in the West Indies. Craddock's task was, perhaps, the most difficult of all. He would not only have to run von Spee to earth but would also have to destroy the enemy raiders in the Caribbean and guard against more German liners running the blockade from American ports.

His first task, however, was to find von Spee's East Asiatic Squadron. And that proved to be a task of considerable difficulty.

Build up to Battle

Jinking slowly southwards, from one island chain to the next, by 30 September von Spee was off Taihiti. There, in his first offensive action, he shelled the French port instillations and, when challenged by the tiny gunboat *Zele*, he promptly sank it. Before the alarm could be telegraphed to the world, he and his ships had disappeared over the horizon.

On 15 October he was joined by the *Dresden* which had left the Caribbean to run the gauntlet down the east coast of South America and through the Magellan Straits into the Pacific. Von Spee's Squadron now consisted of the powerful *Scharnhorst* and *Gneisenau* and the three light cruisers *Leipzig*, *Nürnberg* and *Dresden*.

The effect of von Spee's actions, even of his mere presence in the Pacific, was enough to terrify the governments of Australia and New Zealand. The detached and independently operating *Emden*, *Karlsruhe* and *Königsberg* merely added to

Von Spee's Squadron moored off Valparaiso in 1914, before the outbreak of hostilities. The *Scharnhorst* and *Gneisenau* lie furthest off shore.

the pressure and when they began to sink merchantmen, panic set in. Australia and New Zealand seriously considered suspending the troop convoys bringing ANZAC troops to fight in France until adequate protection could be provided or until von Spee's ships were sunk. Finding and destroying von Spee was now a priority.

Wireless telegraphy was in its early days and not always reliable. However, on 4 October a crackling and static-haunted message from the *Scharnhorst* was intercepted by an Allied WT Station. The *Scharnhorst* it said, was *en route* to Easter Island. It was suddenly and alarmingly clear that von Spee's destination was the coast of South America where, untroubled by Allied warships, he could wreak havoc with the merchant vessels carrying cargoes like meat, grain and copper to a hungry and increasingly anxious Britain. And after that the Atlantic beckoned. Thousands of miles away, at the Admiralty, Winston Churchill consulted with Battenberg, the First Sea Lord, and his Chief of Staff, Sir Frederick Doveton Sturdee. With all his usual imperiousness, Churchill promptly began to change the dispositions of the British ships in the South Atlantic, even though such changes and movements did not really lie within his jurisdiction.

To the analysts advising Churchill at the Admiralty the situation was complex. The Navy now had the doubly difficult task of, firstly, stopping the German East Asiatic Fleet from devastating shipping along the Chilean coast and then preventing von Spee from entering the Atlantic. If the German admiral should ever get into the Atlantic, Churchill and the others reasoned, he would cause untold damage.

A composite postcard from 1914, showing the defenders of Britain and her Empire. Prince Louis of Battenberg, then First Sea Lord, is in the centre of the top row. His successor, Jacky Fisher is pictured alongside him.

Admiral of the Fleet John Arbuthnot "Jacky" Fisher, 1st Baron Fisher, GCB OM GCVO, 1841–1920; First Sea Lord 1904–10 and 1914–15.

In particular there was the River Plate, the outlet for the beef and corn supplies of Argentina and other South American countries. It was crucially important to keep the area safe and free from German influence. But that was not all—far from it. The trade routes to and from North America, all the vast riches of the West African coast—and the military operations in South West Africa—all of them involved the Atlantic and, if von Spee did make it around the Cape, they would lie wide open to the raiders. It did not bear thinking about.

The man to guard the Magellan Straits and bring von Spee to battle had to be Rear Admiral Christopher Craddock, then commanding the West Indian Station.

Craddock was a fifty-two year old Yorkshireman, a natural leader and someone as popular with his crews as von Spee was with his. He was impetuous and dashing, a man who had gone on record as stating that when his time came he hoped he would die either on the hunting field or in action at sea.

When, in due course, orders came through to head for the Falkland Islands, Craddock had mixed feelings. He knew there was a job to do, knew that von Spee and his squadron had to be destroyed. But he also had to leave his three County Class cruisers—the *Suffolk*, *Lancaster* and *Essex*—behind in the West Indies. He handed over command to Admiral Hornby and sailed south, taking with him his new flagship, the recently arrived *Good Hope*, and the light cruiser *Bristol*. Waiting for him off the South American coast were the light cruiser *Glasgow*, a fast ship, ably commanded by John Luce, and the armed merchant cruiser *Otranto*. The old armoured cruiser *Monmouth* had just been detached from home waters and would join him any day.

As well as being a naturally aggressive fighting man, Craddock was also a realist and knew that his new squadron was limited. The modern *Glasgow* was all very well but she was a slight vessel, neither heavily armed nor well armoured,

HMS *Good Hope*, yet another out of date cruiser assigned to protecting the sea lanes. She duly became Kit Craddock's flagship and under his command headed south from the West Indies towards the Falkland Islands.

The fast light cruiser *Glasgow*, the only British ship to fight at both Coronel and the Falklands. Commanded by John Luce, she was the ideal vessel to scout ahead of Craddock's Squadron and give news of the German fleet.

The armed merchant cruiser *Otranto* is seen here before the war and prior to her conversion into an AMC. Her high freeboard and towering superstructure are clearly evident, attributes that made her a liability in any battle situation.

a ship more valuable in a scouting role than in taking a place on the battle line. The AMC *Otranto*, like all such converted passenger ships, would be of little real use against von Spee.

More importantly, Craddock was only too well aware that, unless he was very lucky, in a ship to ship engagement his two old armoured cruisers, the *Good Hope* and *Monmouth*, would have almost no hope against the newer and more powerful *Scharnhorst* and *Gneisenau*. The British ships dated from 1902 and 1903. They were products of bad design with many of their guns mounted in casements far too low to the waterline. As one critic had said, pound for pound more water came in through the gun ports than the number of shells that ever left them. Gunners standing knee deep in swirling foam was not unusual. The total weight of broadside, even if all of their guns were workable—highly unlikely in the seas around the Cape Horn area—was just over 2,000 pounds, approximately half that of the two German cruisers.

The *Good Hope* and *Monmouth* had been built to make 24 knots but that had been many years ago. Now they were considerably slower than their German counterparts. They were also crewed by Reservists, men who had only recently rejoined the ranks. They had received little or no training in modern gunnery techniques and had certainly undergone no gunnery practice. It did not take a genius to see that disaster was staring Craddock in the face.

The *Monmouth* was the final vessel in Craddock's Squadron. Her low gunports can be clearly seen in this early postcard view of the ship.

Churchill knew it, of course, although he could never admit it outright. In his original orders that September, commanding Craddock to head south, he had outlined the reinforcements he was prepared to send:–

> Concentrate a squadron strong enough to meet *Scharnhorst* and *Gneisenau*, making Falkland Islands your coaling base, and leaving sufficient force to deal with *Dresden* and *Karlsruhe*. *Defence* is joining you from the Mediterranean and *Canopus* is now *en route* to Abrolhos. You should keep at least one County Class and *Canopus* with your flagship until *Defence* joins.[6]

When he had a 'superior force,' Churchill went on, Craddock was to search and navigate the Magellan Straits, sailing as far north as Valparaiso if necessary, where he was to find and destroy the German cruisers. Quite what was meant by 'superior force' was never made clear and, anyway, it was not long before the orders were changed.

The *Defence*—a modern armoured cruiser, probably the only vessel in the southern hemisphere capable of matching the German cruisers in both speed and armament—did not come to Craddock and was sent, instead to join Admiral Stoddart at Montevideo where her strength and power would be invaluable in helping to defend the River Plate.

The *Defence*—probably the only vessel in the southern hemisphere that could have matched the two German armoured cruisers—was destined to play no part in the Battle of Coronel but her peripheral role as a potential addition to Craddock's force made her an important component of the tragic affair.

Churchill and all of the staff at the Admiralty were haunted by the nightmare that von Spee would somehow manage to evade Craddock, sail around the Cape and cause chaos to British shipping in the South Atlantic. In their eyes, the need to maintain effective Squadrons on both coasts of South America was paramount.

The battleship *Canopus*, Churchill considered, was sufficient to provide Craddock with all the power and strength he needed:–

> The old battleship, with her heavy armour and artillery, was in fact a citadel around which all our cruisers in those waters could find absolute security.[7]

As so often before—and later—Churchill was deluding himself. A 'citadel' the *Canopus* was certainly not. She was a pre-Dreadnought battleship armed with four 12 inch guns, twelve 6 inch and numerous secondary weapons.

Yet these guns were all of early vintage and were greatly outranged by the armament of both von Spee's modern armoured cruisers, supposedly of a smaller calibre. Like the *Good Hope*, her gun crews were Reservists with little training and, having just rejoined the Fleet, no experience of firing their weapons, not even in practice.

She was old and slow, having been designed to make just 18 knots, but now her potential speed was unsure. Until recently she had been mothballed under Care and Maintenance conditions in Milford Haven and was due for

The old battleship *Canopus*, a vessel that Winston Churchill insisted would be Craddock's citadel, was dispatched from the Third (or Reserve) Fleet as a reinforcement. Slow, cumbersome, crewed by Reservists, she arrived at the Falkland Islands too late to be of any real assistance.

the breakers yard in 1915. The war changed all of that and she was hurriedly brought back into service.

The British admiral, the man 'on the spot,' was nothing if not a realist and the Admiralty's fear of a German squadron establishing itself on the eastern coast of South America was reciprocated by Craddock. The addition of *Canopus* to his motley array of ships did not allay his fears in the slightest. On 8 October he signalled the following message:–

> ... should the concentrated British force sent from South East Coast be evaded in the Pacific, which is not impossible, and get behind the enemy, the latter could destroy Falklands, English Bank and Abrolhos coaling bases in turn with little to stop them, and with British ships unable to follow up owing to want of coal, enemy might possibly reach West Indies.[8]

He received no satisfactory answer although he did continue to push for *Defence* to be detached from Stoddart's fleet and sent to join his squadron. Admiral Craddock duly arrived at the Falkland Islands, sending *Glasgow* to scout northwards up the Chilean coast. Then he settled down to await the arrival of his 'citadel,' the old battleship *Canopus* on which Winston Churchill seemed to set so much store.

3

Hunting the Raiders—
Liners at War

Armed merchant cruisers may not have been particularly successful but the mere presence of German ships around the convoy or regular trade routes caused serious tremors in the Admiralty. And there was always the gnawing concern that worse was to come. The Hamburg-Amerika Line alone had several hundred ships that could all be converted into AMC's—if they managed to get past the blockade of the Royal Navy.

Despite a virtual 'siege' of the German and American coasts during the first few months of the war, a handful of German liners did actually manage to run the blockade. Duly converted into armed merchant cruisers, these vessels caused considerable anxiety and wrought serious damage before they were either hunted down or fled to the security of neutral ports.

The *Kaiser Wilhelm der Gross* had once been the fastest ship afloat and in 1897 had claimed the famous Blue Riband for the quickest crossing of the Atlantic. On the night of 4 August 1914 she had slipped out of Bremenhaven, armed with six 4 inch guns, her hull painted black, and moved carefully up the Norwegian coast. After sinking a trawler—one of the first British losses of the war—she swept past Iceland and down into the South Atlantic.

Four British merchantmen fell to the *Kaiser Wilhelm der Grosse* and her courteous commander, Captain Raymann, who invariably released the enemy crews once he had relieved them of their ships and cargoes. It might have been the gentlemanly thing to do but such a practice was not really the way to wage war as it invariably told the hunting British cruisers exactly where the *Kaiser Wilhelm der Grosse* was operating.

Finally, low on coal and determined to rest his crew, Raymann moored off the Spanish possession of Rio de Oro on the African coast to re-fuel. Courteous or not, Raymann was a pragmatist and he deliberately flouted the laws of neutrality by staying off the port for nearly two weeks. In the end his prolonged stay was his undoing as it was here that the raider was surprised by the cruiser *Highflyer* from Admiral John de Robeck's Finisterre Squadron. Despite being within Spanish territorial waters the *Highflyer* immediately challenged the German raider and an unequal battle began.

The shattered hull of the armed merchant cruiser *Kaiser Wilhelm der Grosse*, once one of the finest passenger ships in the world, lies off the beach at Rio de Oro. Her cruise as a raider had been short-lived.

The cruiser *Highflyer* which cornered and sank the *Kaiser Wilhelm der Grosse* off the west coast of Africa.

The action lasted for just over an hour. *The Kaiser Wilhem der Grosse* was battered by the 6 inch guns of the British cruiser, her elegant panelling and decking splintered to fragments. Raymann and eighty-one crew managed to swim ashore to internment by the Spaniards while their once-beautiful liner heeled over and sank.

Liners at Bay

The *Kronprinz Wilhelm* had managed to slip out of New York harbour the day before war began, her peacetime commander Grahn being replaced by Naval Officer Captain Thierfelder. In the West Indies she rendezvoused with the cruiser *Karlsruhe* but in the middle of taking on board guns and ammunition, the two raiders were surprised by the *Suffolk* from Craddock's West Indian Squadron and forced to hurry off, in opposite directions. The British went after the cruiser which, being one of the speediest vessels afloat, soon outran them and disappeared.

Once out of danger, Captain Thierfelder began to convert his liner for war service, using the saloon as a bunker for coal and nailing mattresses to bulkheads to protect the crew from shell splinters.[9] Then began months of lonely cruising,

The cruiser *Suffolk* had been part of Kit Craddock's Squadron in the West Indies but he was forced to leave her behind when he headed south in search of von Spee. The *Suffolk* almost intercepted the *Karlsruhe* but lost the faster German ship when the raider quickly took to her heels.

searching for prizes. Pickings were slim and when Thierfelder did once encounter a Russian tramp steamer he let her pass, unmolested, as her captain explained that the ship was his only way of making a living. Thierfelder thought up many ingenious ways of keeping his crew fit and happy during their lonely cruise. These included building a homemade movie theatre, rowing boat races around the ship and driving two motor cars, plundered from a captured merchantman, around the deck. Despite his efforts—and despite the award of one hundred Iron Crosses to the crew—depression and, inevitably, sickness began to set in.

The *Kronprinz Wilhelm* took fourteen prizes in all, one of which she tried to sink by ramming it—the move failed and the liner sprang a leak which the crew had to repair by pouring concrete into the liner's bows. In the spring of 1915 she was ordered to make for home. Despite being intercepted by two British cruisers, the liner managed to escape and remain at large. Finally, Thierfelder, realising he would never be able to make it back to Germany, was able to take his ship into American territory in Chesapeake Bay where she was promptly interned. She had completed a 250 day cruise and sunk 58,000 tons of Allied shipping.

The *Cormoran* was neither so lucky nor so successful. Operating in the Pacific she was, almost from the beginning of her career, hampered by a chronic lack of fuel. In the early days of the war she had been with von Spee's Squadron at Pagan and the Mariana Islands, the fleet also including the AMC *Prinz Eitel Friedrich*. Then, along with the *Prinz Eitel Friedrich*, she was ordered by the admiral to attack trade in the Australian waters while von Spee himself sailed off towards the South American coast.

It was not a particularly successful cruise. Both the *Cormoran* and the *Prinz Eitel Friedrich* were desperately short on coal and neither could find enemy vessels carrying enough of the precious fuel to fill their bunkers. They were eventually forced to abandon the mission, the *Prinz Eitel Friedrich* rejoining von Spee at Mas a Fuera and the *Cormoran* docking at Guam where she was soon forced to seek internment.

The *Prinz Eitel Friedrich* under Captain Thierichsens, remained at large in the Pacific. Von Spee, before setting off for Coronel and the Falklands, had ordered her to continue raiding in the hope of convincing the British that the East Asiatic Squadron was still at large on the west coast of South America. But after the German defeat at the Falklands, Thierichsens realised it was a forlorn mission. He was alone and decided to make for home.

Despite the weather conditions he rounded the Horn and sailed north. Deciding not to risk the blockade, he remained at sea for several weeks, taking three or four prizes. With food running out and no hope of being re-supplied, however, Thierichsens finally came to rest at Newport in the USA. In March 1915 his ship was interned, her cruise over.

The Carmania and the Cap Trafalgar

The British response to the threat of the German armed merchant cruisers was to equip, sail and fight some of their own.

When the Cunard liner *Carmania* docked at Liverpool in August 1914 she was the epitome of the luxurious ocean liner. Within a few weeks she was transformed. Her hull, upper works and funnels were painted dull grey and eight 4.7 inch guns mounted on her upper deck. Command was given to Captain Noel Grant of the Royal Navy but her peacetime commander, Captain Barr, stayed on board to advise Grant about the idiosyncrasies of the *Carmania* and keep a wary eye on his ship. Crewed by Reservists and a mixture of volunteers and trawlermen, she was assigned to the fleet of Admiral Craddock, then still in the West Indies.

On the morning of 14 September the *Carmania* was dispatched by Craddock to Trinidada to search for the raider *Dresden* who, it was suspected, was lurking in the area. What she found was the stark outline of a huge ocean-going liner, the German armed merchant cruiser *Cap Trafalgar*, a triple-screw steamer, originally run on the South American route. She was a ship that was:–

> … a floating hotel—she had also, with great foresight, been built strongly enough to carry heavy armament of guns in case of emergency.[10]

The *Carmania* was the smaller of the two vessels but her armament was almost equal to that of the German ship and Captain Grant decided to fight. As soon as the *Carmania* was spotted, the *Cap Trafalgar* cast off and sped away to the south. However, quickly realising that the *Carmania* was alone, the *Cap Trafalgar* put over her helm and turned to meet the enemy.

To begin with the German fire was the more accurate and shells soon began to rain down onto the super-structure of the *Carmania*. Fire broke out on her bridge and, with the water mains cut, Captain Grant was forced to abandon the bridge and con the ship from aft. The *Carmania* was also making her shots count, however, and soon it was observed that the *Cap Trafalgar* had taken a decided list to starboard. Desperate to avoid the British broadsides, the *Cap Trafalgar* closed to within 3,000 yards, a mistake as her guns could have out-ranged the *Carmania*'s by several thousand yards. It was something the German commander clearly did not know. Having closed the range, the Germans opened fire with Maxim guns, causing many casualties amongst the fire-fighting British crew. At such close range, however, the British gunners could hardly miss and they continued to pour shells into the hull of the enemy liner. As Captain Grant controlled the ship and the fighting, so her peace time commander, Captain Barr, took charge of the fire control parties.

At last, the *Cap Trafalgar* turned away, her captain dead and the crew possibly attempting to beach the giant ship on the island. It was a vain exercise as, with the sea pouring into her hull, she came to a dead stop in the water. A few lifeboats were lowered but:–

The end of the German armed merchant cruiser *Cap Trafalgar*, an illustration by the marine artist W. L. Wyllie.

Crew members survey the damage to the British AMC *Carmania* which sank the *Cap Trafalgar* on 14 September 1914. It had been a close run thing with the British ship sustaining serious damage.

Cap Trafalgar … a little later, turned right on her beam ends and as the sea dashed over her decks the great liner slowly righted herself. The masthead flags still flew in brave defiance, the eagle and iron cross fluttering for one brief moment among the clouds of steam and black smoke belching upwards to the sky. Then the whole fabric sank, with the deadly sounds of bursting hatches and rushing water.[11]

Nearby German colliers picked up survivors but the crew of the *Carmania* had enough trouble trying to save their own ship. Seventy nine shells had struck her during the battle and Captain Grant was plagued by the fear that the *Dresden* was lurking just over the horizon. Accordingly, he ordered a course for the Albrohos Rocks, hoping to encounter a British ship soon. Early the following afternoon smoke was sighted on the horizon— the *Bristol* had arrived to escort the damaged armed merchant cruiser back to base.

The Mysterious End of the Karlsruhe

The *Karlsruhe*, along with the *Dresden*, was one of the fastest light cruisers in the world, a ship capable of making an amazing 28 knots, a modern and efficient fighting machine. When war broke out she was in the Caribbean, keeping watch on the safety of German nationals caught up in the Mexican Civil War.

In the last few days of peace Captain Köhler of the *Dresden* and Captain Lüdecke of the *Karlsruhe* exchanged commands. It was originally intended for Lüdecke to take *Dresden* home to Germany for a refit but the declaration of war changed the German plans.

While Lüdecke immediately sailed south, Köhler and the *Karlsruhe* remained in the West Indies where the pickings were rich and the weather fine, if decidedly dangerous. Over the next few months the mere mention of the *Karlsruhe*—or, for that matter, the other lone German raiders, *Dresden* and *Emden*—was enough to send ship owners and captains white with fear. Thanks to the tireless patrolling of Craddock and his cruisers, and actions like the fight between *Cap Trafalgar* and *Carmania* which caused the attendant colliers to scatter, by the middle of September 1914 the German network of coaling vessels had been virtually destroyed. As a result, raiders like the *Karlsruhe* were desperately short of fuel.

Nevertheless, Captain Köhler duly took his ship south where she came to rest in Orange Bay on the southern tip of Chile. She had just over ten tons of coal in her bunkers. Obtaining ready supplies of coal had now become a major problem for the raider.

A new network of coaling ships—using Hamburg-Sud-Amerika liners like the *Rio Negro* and *Asuncion* that had been in Argentinian ports when war broke out, thereby avoiding the British blockade—was set up. And when Köhler captured the steamer *Strathroy*, carrying 5,000 tons of best Welsh coal, it made him free from fuel worries for the immediate future.[12]

The *Karlsruhe*, once the fastest cruiser in the world, was sunk when a mysterious explosion ripped her apart. She was on her way to bombard Barbados and there is still intense speculation about the cause of her demise. This photograph is of *Karlsruhe* coaling in San Juan, Puerto Rico, 9 August 1914

Craddock, sailing south as per Admiralty orders, totally missed the *Karlsruhe* which, together with the captured *Strathroy*, was then hiding in an anchorage at Lavandeira Reefs. And once Craddock was past, the *Karlsruhe* was free to emerge and begin raiding operations in earnest. Half a dozen enemy prizes were taken, ships carrying coal, grain and meat, before Köhler returned to Lavandeira Reefs to overhaul his engines. Then, laden with so much coal that his decks were nearly awash, he set off again. More prizes were taken and, more importantly, the searching British cruisers of Admiral Stoddart's squadron were avoided.

So many British and neutral ships were captured over the next few weeks that it sometimes seemed as if the *Karlsruhe* had wings. So great was the fear of this fast and elusive ship that Churchill in the Admiralty decided to attach the armoured cruiser *Defence* to Stoddart's searching squadron on a permanent basis instead of despatching her to where she would have done a lot more good, with Admiral Craddock in the south.

Stoddart was not to know it but he was searching an empty sea as Köhler had already left the Atlantic, heading once more for the Caribbean. His plan was to shell Barbados and Martinique, an operation that would have been as depressing for British morale as it would have been heart lifting for the Germans. The *Karlsruhe* had already sunk over 75,000 tons of Allied shipping. This, Köhler reckoned, would be the icing on the cake.

Sonderkarte: Die Operationen des Kleinen Kreuzers „Karlsruhe" vom 30. A...

Zu: Der Kreuzerkrieg in den ausländischen Gewässern, Band 2.

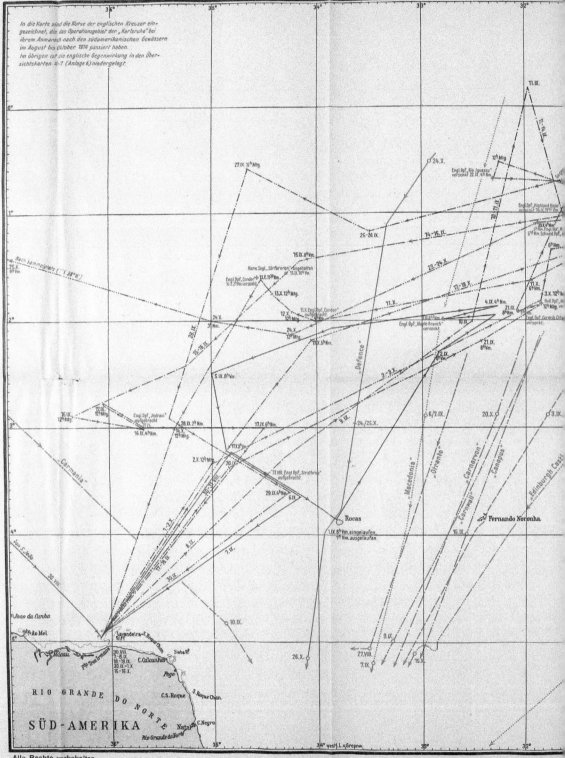

In die Karte sind die Kurse der englischen Kreuzer ein-
gezeichnet, die das Operationsgebiet der „Karlsruhe" bei
ihrem Anmarsch nach den südamerikanischen Gewässern
im August bis Oktober 1914 passiert haben.
Im übrigen ist die englische Gegenwirkung in den Über-
sichtskarten 4-7 (Anlage 6) niedergelegt.

RIO GRANDE DO NORTE

SÜD-AMERIKA

Maßstab 1 : 2000000

Anlage 5.

St. Paul Rocks

"Carnarvon"
"Canopus"
"Cornwall"
"Good Hope" z.R.
"Edinburgh Castle"

21.X.
21.IX.
8.IX.
24.IX.
IX.6.
IX.
23.X.8 Vm.
9.X.8 Vm.
10.X. 9 Vm.
22.X. 8 Vm.
Engl.Dpf."Pruth"
Schwed.Dpf."Alland" angehalten
5.X.8 Vm.
6.X.8 Vm.
Engl.Dpf."Lynrowan" 1.X.8 Vm aufgebracht 3 Nm.versenkt.
Engl.Dpf."Niceto de Larrinaga" 6.X.3½ Nm.aufgebracht, 7.X. 1.30 Vm.versenkt.

Engl.Dpf."Cervantes" aufgehr. 12. Nm.versenkt

"Cornwall"
3.IX.
"Good Hope"
14.X.
4.X.
"Macedonia u. Orama"

Liste der vom Kl.Krz."Karlsruhe"angehaltenen Dampfer :

18.Aug.	4.50 Nm.	Engl.Dpf. "Bowes Castle"	7.30 Nm.versenkt
31. "	4h Nm.	" " "Strathrey"	25.IX.versenkt
3.Sept.	5h Vm.	" " "Maple Branch"	5.45 Nm.versenkt
14. "	5.30 Vm.	" " "Highland Hope"	11.45 Vm.versenkt
15. "	10h Vm.	Norw.Segl. "Sarfareren"	entlassen
17. "	mittags	Engl.Dpf. "Indrani"	9.XI.versenkt
21. "	9h Vm.	Ital.Dpf. "Maria"	mittags versenkt
21. "	2.45 Nm.	Engl.Dpf. "Cornish City"	7.30 Nm.versenkt
22. "	6h Vm.	Ital.Dpf. "Ascaro"	entlassen
22. "	6.40 Vm.	Engl.Dpf. "Rio Iguassu"	4h Nm.versenkt
22. "	7h Vm.	Schwed.Dpf. "Princ.Jageborg"	entlassen
5.Okt.	5h Nm.	Engl.Dpf. "Farn"	12.15 S.laon eingelaufen
6. "	3h Nm.	" " "Niceto de Larrinaga	7.X. 1.30 Vm.versenkt
7. "	8h Vm.	" " "Lynrowan"	3h Nm.versenkt
8. "	7h Vm.	" " "Cervantes"	12.30 Nm.versenkt
8/9. "	12h Nchts	" " "Pruth"	9.X. 10.9 Vm.versenkt
9. "	3h Vm.	Span.Peseldpf."Cadiz"	entlassen
10. "	3h Vm.	Norw.Dpf. "Bergenhus"	"
11. "	4h Vm.	Engl.Dpf. "Condor"	14.X. 2h Vm.versenkt
18. "	11h Vm.	" " "Glanton"	5.30 Nm.versenkt
22. "	10.30 Nm.	Schwed.Dpf. "Alland"	entlassen
23. "	6h Vm.	Engl.Dpf. "Hurstdale"	9h Nm.versenkt
23. "	6.45 Nm.	Schwed.Dpf. "Annie Johnson"	entlassen
26. "	11h Vm.	Engl.Dpf. "Van Dyck"	28.X.6.30 Vm.versenkt
27. "	11.30 Nm.	" " "Royal Scaptre"	entlassen

Zeichenerklärung:

Kurs vom 30.VIII. 7.30 Vm.bis 7.IX. 11h Vm.
" " 8.IX. 8.30 Vm.bis 18.IX. 9h Vm.
" " 19.IX. 5h Vm.bis 30.IX. 11.30 Vm.
" " 7.X. 5h Nm.bis 15.X. 8.30 Vm.
" " 16.X. 5h Vm.bis 25.X. 9h Vm.

○ = Angehaltene Dampfer
● = Aufgebrachte Dampfer
✛ = Versenkte Dampfer

Verlag von E. S. Mittler & Sohn, Berlin.

A contemporary German chart. The legend top left reads: On the chart are marked the courses of the English cruisers which passed the waters through which the *Karlsruhe* sailed on her way out to South American operations area from August until October 1914. From Erich Raeder: *Der Kreuzerkrieg in den ausländischen Gewässern*, volume 2. Berlin 1923.

Die Operationen des Kleinen Kreuzers „Karlsruh

(einschließlich Rückfahrt der Besatzung auf Dampfer „Rio Negro").

Geogr. lith. Anst. u. Steindr. v. C. L. Keller, Berlin S.

Verlag von E. S. Mittler & Sohn, Berlin.

The operation of the cruiser SMS *Karlsruhe*
from Erich Raeder: *Der Kreuzerkrieg in den
ausländischen Gewässern*, Volume 2. Berlin 1923.

At the end of October, when the *Karlsruhe* was barely 200 miles short of Barbados, a sudden and devastating explosion rocked the ship which immediately broke into two halves. The front part quickly sank, taking 200 crewmen— including Captain Köhler—to the bottom. The rear section remained afloat for half an hour, enough time for the attending colliers to pick up 150 survivors.

What happened to cause the explosion has never been fully explained. A technical fault? Sabotage? A rogue mine?—though this is highly unlikely. Her real importance to Germany lay, not in the ships she might sink but in her propaganda value.

Fear of the raider was like an infectious disease in the shipping world and was something on which the Germans wished to capitalise as much as possible. There was no way they would admit that the *Karlsruhe* had been sunk and so news of her destruction was kept hidden for several months, the German Admiralty even sending fake signals to the supposedly still patrolling raider. Not until survivors on board the liner/collier *Rio Negro* managed to slip down the Norwegian coast back into Germany did the news break. By then, of course, events in the southern hemisphere had moved on apace.

4

Coronel—Disaster in the Pacific

The Search for von Spee

On 18 October 1914, the very day that Rear Admiral von Spee sailed from Easter Island, HMS *Glasgow* was heading south towards the port of Coronel where her Captain, John Luce, was expecting to rendezvous with his commander-in-chief, Admiral Sir Christopher Craddock. Several weeks earlier Luce had been despatched from the Falkland Islands up the coast towards Valparaiso to search for the German East Asiatic Squadron. He had drawn a blank—von Spee was there, somewhere in the Pacific, but for the moment he could not be found.

Craddock knew that the German ships were in the area. A few weeks earlier, when the *Good Hope* had put into Orange Bay, he had found evidence that an enemy light cruiser—in all probability the *Dresden*—had been there before him.

His forces were now concentrated on Port Stanley in the Falkland Islands, waiting for the arrival of the battleship *Canopus* but he was still concerned about the strength of his squadron, even with the supposed citadel of the *Canopus* to back him up. He needed the power of the *Defence* to make his force anything like equal to the Germans. On 11 October he sent a telegram to the Admiralty, reporting the *Dresden*'s presence, but adding an almost desperate postscript:–

With reference to Admiralty telegram No 74, does '*Defence*' join my command?[13]

The answer was an emphatic 'No.' As far as Churchill and the Admiralty were concerned the addition of the *Canopus* would be enough. A Japanese Squadron, including the battleship *Hizen*, was reported as beginning to move down the Pacific coast of South America and between these and Craddock's ships, hopefully, von Spee would be pincered and crushed like a walnut.

In fact the Japanese task force was still in the process of assembling. It would take weeks for them to combine into an effective fighting unit and even then the likelihood of encountering von Spee in the vastness of the Pacific must have been one in a thousand. The Admiralty either did not know the facts or carefully avoided them.

In October 1914 Kit Craddock took the *Good Hope* and the rest of his Squadron around the Cape to hunt for von Spee in the Pacific. He found a great deal of evidence that the German ships had been there, in the places where he was searching, but for a long while saw no trace of his opposite number.

And then, on 18 October—surely a fateful date for Kit Craddock—he received a signal from his 'citadel,' the old battleship. She would be at least a week late in arriving at the Falkland Islands and, importantly, due to the state of her engines was not able to make anything like 15 knots. Craddock immediately informed the Admiralty but his telegram was ambiguous:–

> I trust circumstances will enable me to force an action, but fear that, strategically, owing to *Canopus*, the speed of my Squadron cannot exceed 12 knots.[14]

Was Craddock intending to take *Canopus* with him into the Pacific? The telegram could certainly be read that way. In the event Churchill and the men at the Admiralty chose to understand that this was what Craddock was going to do. In making such an assumption, they tragically mis-read not only Craddock's message but also his character. On 27 October he sent a further signal to the Admiralty and, having carefully buried all his medals and decorations in the garden of the governor's house at Port Stanley, took the *Good Hope* around the Cape into the Pacific Ocean:–

> I consider that owing to the slow speed of *Canopus* it is impossible to find and destroy the enemy's squadron. Have therefore ordered *Defence* to join me after

calling for orders at Montevideo. Shall employ *Canopus* on necessary work of convoying colliers.[15]

The telegram threw the Admiralty, where the mercurial Jacky Fisher was in the process of replacing Prince Louis of Battenberg as First Sea Lord, into confusion. Craddock had no authority to order *Defence* to join him and his order was immediately countermanded. Yet nothing was said about his decision to relegate *Canopus* to convoy duties, thereby implying approval or acceptance. Whether it was overlooked or was an issue that was meant to be addressed later is not known. Mixed messages and total confusion—all part of the tragic build up to the Battle of Coronel.

When, at the beginning of November, the Admiralty received news from the British Consul in Valparaiso that von Spee's Squadron had been sighted off the Chilean coast, Churchill and Fisher gave an almost audible sigh of relief. The German fleet was still on the west coast and Stoddart at Montevideo was, for the

HMS *Carnarvon* was one of six Devonshire-class armoured cruisers built for the Royal Navy. She was commissioned into the Navy in 1905 and assigned to the 3rd Cruiser Squadron of the Mediterranean Fleet and was transferred to the 2nd Cruiser Squadron of the Atlantic Fleet in 1907. She was assigned to the reserve Third Fleet in 1909 and became flagship of the 5th Cruiser Squadron of the reserve Second Fleet in 1912. HMS *Carnarvon* was scrapped in 1921.

moment at least, quite safe. It was time for another change of mind. Churchill, always searching for the fine phrase, and clearly seeking to avoid any blame either for the Admiralty or for himself, later commented:–

> We telegraphed to Admiral Craddock once more reiterating the instructions about the *Canopus—Defence* has been ordered to join your flag with all dispatch. *Glasgow* should find or keep in touch with the enemy. You should keep in touch with *Glasgow* concentrating the rest of your squadron, including *Canopus*. It is important you should effect your junction with *Defence* at earliest possible moment. But we were already talking to the void.[16]

Off to Coronel

Attempting to obey the original Admiralty instructions to hunt down and destroy the German forces in the Pacific, the impetuous Kit Craddock had grown tired of waiting. In the last days of October he headed out from Port Stanley into a wild Cape storm that whipped up the sea around his ships into a fury and sent spray arching back over their superstructure. In continuing gales and winds that threw a mixture of snow, rain and hail at the British squadron, they dutifully searched the long fiords that dotted the coastline and at times split up in order to explore more effectively. Their searching was in vain and in the end the squadron re-united to continue the hunt.

Flying his flag in *Good Hope*, Craddock moved steadily northwards. With him, now, were the *Monmouth*, and the AMC *Otranto* while the *Glasgow* was usually scouting ahead of the squadron. It was hardly a strong force and Craddock, facing what was, potentially at least, a vastly superior enemy, must have known that he was unlikely to return. Why else would he bury his medals and give the Governor of the Falkland Islands a sealed packet to be sent to the Admiralty in the event of his death? Kit Craddock was, in many respects, a romantic. The grand gesture was in his soul. And yet he was also a realist. He would do his duty, regardless of the cost—that was the way of things with men like him, products of the old Navy with Victorian ideals and values ever present. The two stances were not diametrically opposed. Indeed, they meshed easily together in Craddock's character. And that character was what led him on towards his death.

He did not have, as has sometimes been suggested, a death wish or a premonition of oncoming failure and disaster. But he knew that his chances of success were limited, hence his decision to bury his medals—the grand gesture in action—before setting out to do his duty and meet his fate, whatever that might be. Craddock's character was a weakness, a fatal weakness in a leader about to go into combat. When the odds were evenly stacked, there was no major problem. When faced by an opponent like Admiral von Spee and when equipped with a markedly inferior force, it could lead in only one direction—to disaster.

Craddock was a realist who knew that his ships were out-classed but he was determined to do his duty. If needed he would die in the attempt.

Spread out in a line, fifteen miles apart, Craddock's squadron ploughed doggedly onwards, the *Canopus* and her colliers some 300 miles behind him. Just after midday on 1 November Luce and the *Glasgow* were spotted, steaming hastily towards the British Squadron. They brought important news.

Glasgow had picked up a German wireless message from the light cruiser *Leipzig* which, it seemed, was operating independently of von Spee's main force. Craddock immediately saw that here was an opportunity to pick off the cruiser and he increased speed to bring about the confrontation before the *Leipzig* could rejoin her squadron.

Unfortunately, von Spee was hell bent on the same mission. He had received news from German merchant shipping in the port of Coronel that *Glasgow* had, only that morning, come in with mail and, recalling the *Leipzig*, he sped south in the hope of intercepting her before she could rejoin the *Good Hope* and *Monmouth*. Two forces, drawn together like magnet and steel filings, were now irrevocably being brought together.

At 4.30 p.m., with the weather squally and the sea wild, Luce's lookouts on the *Glasgow* reported smoke to the north. The moment of confrontation had arrived.

S. M. S. „Leipzig" am 8. 12. 14 im Seegefecht
bei den Falklandsinseln gesunken

The first real evidence that von Spee's Squadron was close came when the *Glasgow* picked up radio messages from the light cruiser *Leipzig* which was operating independently close to the Chilean coast. Craddock hurried north, hoping to catch her alone before she could re-join von Spee.

The Battle of Coronel

The German ships were widely scattered but von Spee, spotting British smoke at the same time as he was seen by his opponents, realised what fate had conveniently laid in front of him. He immediately ordered his squadron to close up and increase speed, confident now of destroying not just the *Glasgow* but the whole British squadron.

Von Spee knew only too well that until the sun began to sink below the horizon he was at a disadvantage. With the British ships to the west of him, von Spee and his cruisers were clearly visible while his own gunners would be dazzled by the rays of the low setting sun. But once the sun disappeared—just after 7.00 p.m. at that time of year—the advantage would swing the other way. Then the British ships would be outlined against the after glow of the sunset and the horizon, making perfect targets for the German gunners. The light from the moon, almost full, would simply add to the British vulnerability.

Von Spee, tactician to the last, knew he had to delay the action. He therefore used his superior speed to veer off whenever the British came too close, keeping out of range and all the time putting himself between Craddock and the coast:–

The wind was south, force 6, and the sea high, so that I had to be careful not to be manoeuvred into the lee position. The course chosen helped to cut off the enemy from the neutral coast.[17]

Craddock tried desperately to close the range but von Spee had the advantage of speed and weather conditions. Waves were pounding the *Good Hope* and the sun slid slowly below the horizon. At last, knowing he had lost the sun, Kit Craddock sent his final valiant message to the *Canopus*—'I am going to attack the enemy now'—and turned due south in order to prevent the waves hammering him so badly on the beam. Even so, the lower gun ports of both the *Good Hope* and the *Monmouth* were shipping water and were totally unworkable, thus taking out a large part of his fire power. The situation for Craddock looked increasingly grim, even at this early stage of the action. And then, just after 7.00 p.m., at a range of 12,000 yards, the *Scharnhorst* opened fire.

In what was a really remarkable example of gunnery—small wonder the *Scharnhorst* had once won the German Navy gunnery championship—the German crews were immediately successful. The *Good Hope* was straddled and, with the third salvo, was struck on the forward 9.2 inch gun, the blast destroying the turret and the gun crew inside. A sheet of flame shot skywards, the raging flames and the subsequent illumination making the task even easier for the German gunners.

Craddock had ordered *Otranto* out of line almost before the battle began. Her high freeboard and unarmoured decks would have been easy targets for the crack German gunners and so she pulled out of the battle line and reluctantly headed south. The *Monmouth* took up position behind the flagship, *Glasgow* ploughing resolutely along behind her.

It was always an uneven contest. Neither *Good Hope* nor *Monmouth* could use their lower deck armament in the wild sea and with the German ships shrouded by the darkness of night there was, literally, nothing to aim at. For a long time the only target *Glasgow*'s gunners could identify were the flashes of the enemy guns.

All the while the German shells were roaring down onto the decks of the two armoured cruisers. And their shooting was excellent. Von Spee gradually closed the range and soon both the leading British ships were a mass of twisted wreckage. *Monmouth* took a full broadside from the *Gneisenau* and, with her bridge consumed by fire, she lurched to starboard and began to lose way.

By 7.30 p.m., less than an hour after firing began, both *Good Hope* and *Monmouth* were little more than blazing hulks, their decks just heaps of twisted metal, their sides ripped open in huge rents through which raging fires were clearly visible. Then the British flagship slowly turned to port, towards the German line, and for a while it seemed as if Craddock was trying to ram the enemy and take *Scharnhorst* or *Gneisenau* with him to whatever version of Viking Valhalla he was about to enter. *Gneisenau* promptly switched aim from *Monmouth* to the *Good Hope* and as her salvos hit home the old cruiser stopped dead in the water. Nobody actually witnessed the end but soon after

The Battle of Coronel was short and sharp. With her third salvo the *Scharnhorst* scored a direct hit on the forward turret of the *Good Hope*, totally destroying the gun and sending a sheet of flame high into the air. From then on it was only a matter of time.

The AMC *Otranto* in her wartime colours. Craddock ordered her out of the battle line at the beginning of the action and she fled south to the Falkland Islands.

7.45 p.m. the *Good Hope* exploded in a sheet of flame. Clearly the raging fires had reached her magazine. And then she slipped, almost peacefully, below the waves. Von Spee later wrote that the disaster appeared like:–

> … a splendid firework display against the dark sky. The glowing white flames, mingled with bright green stars, shot up to a great height.[18]

How Kit Craddock died will never be known. Killed by the exploding magazine or drowned in the icy waters, it hardly matters. He had achieved his wish to die in action, sadly and tragically taking 800 men with him. There were no survivors.

The *Glasgow* had been engaged by the three enemy light cruisers—and, for a while, by the *Gneisenau*—taking five shell hits and, in her turn, firing effectively at the enemy. But it was soon clear to Captain Luce that the battle was lost. Visibility had become so poor, thanks to rain squalls and heavy seas, that for the moment there was a lull in the action.

Luce came up to the burning *Monmouth* but quickly realised he could do nothing to aid her—or the remnants of her crew. He received no answer to his message asking if he could do anything for the crippled ship. He had to warn the *Canopus* and *Otranto* and take news of the disaster to the outside world.

Sick at heart, the crew of *Glasgow* watched the wallowing and helpless *Monmouth* for some minutes, then the helm was put over and *Glasgow* sped away. The burning cruiser, flames glowing brightly against the night sky, was a sight that none of those on board would ever forget.

As the moon rose the light cruiser *Nürnberg* came upon the stricken *Monmouth*. If Captain Brand of the British armoured cruiser was still alive, he showed no

As darkness closed in the light cruiser *Nürnberg* came across the shattered hull of the *Monmouth*. She was dead in the water, having been hit by a salvo from the *Gneisenau*, but her colours were still flying and the *Nürnberg* had no option other than to give her the *coup de grâce*.

inclination to pull down the ship's colours and surrender. Such an action was not in the tradition of the Royal Navy. Lieutenant Otto Spee, son of the German Admiral, was on the *Nürnberg* and, after the battle, wrote about the *Monmouth*'s last moments:–

> She had a list of about ten degrees to port. As we came nearer she heeled still more, so that she could no longer use her guns on the side turned towards us. We opened fire at short range. It was terrible for me to have to fire on the poor fellow who was no longer able to defend himself. But the colours were still flying and when we ceased fire for several minutes, he did not haul them down. So we ran up for a fresh attack and caused him to capsize by our gun fire.[19]

Far away to the south the crew of the *Glasgow* saw flashes on the horizon and they knew, without being told, that they marked the end of the *Monmouth*. Like the *Good Hope*, she sank with all hands. The sea and wind, now approaching Gale Force 8, were too strong for the *Nürnberg* to lower boats and search for survivors and Captain von Schonberg, seeing smoke on the horizon, knew that he had to rejoin his squadron as quickly as possible.

Sailing independently, *Glasgow* and *Otranto* continued to head south, back towards the Falkland Islands. Luckily for *Glasgow* three of the shells that had hit her during the battle failed to explode. The crew managed to shore up the only serious damage she had incurred and there was little or no loss of speed. The *Glasgow* finally entered Port Stanley harbour on 6 November in time to help the residents of the colony prepare the town for the assault and landing that was hourly expected. Everyone, naval ratings and inhabitants of Port Stanley prepared to sell their lives dearly.

5

The Aftermath—
Von Spee's Triumph

With victory assured, Admiral von Spee left his light cruisers to search for the remnants of Craddock's Squadron and headed for Valparaiso. The city was home to a substantial German colony and, as the rumours of his success began to spread, something of a spectacular, if impromptu, Triumph in the old Roman style began to take place.

Hundreds of people thronged the waterfront of this neutral port, British and Germans alike, all waiting for definite news of the battle's outcome. Then the *Scharnhorst* and *Gneisenau* hove into view and the rumours could no longer be discounted. The battle had resulted in victory for the Fatherland. Germans in the crowd cheered von Spee to the echo, the British slunk away to their clubs where they thought long and hard on their defeat.

The two reactions were understandable. Britain had not lost a major sea battle for over a hundred years—until now. In the wake of the disaster, British trade off the Chilean coast was abruptly ended. In contrast, German merchant vessels began to appear with seeming impunity. It was, so these South American Germans believed, the beginning of the end for British domination of the seas.

Von Spee himself was much more realistic and restrained. When offered flowers by one ecstatic female admirer he responded with the curt words 'They will do for my grave.' Although his ships had sustained no damage at Coronel, he knew that the British would not take such a defeat lying down. If he had felt hunted before, now he knew that his choices were severely limited:–

> I cannot reach Germany; we possess no other secure harbour; I must plough the seas of the world doing as much mischief as I can, till my ammunition is exhausted, or till a foe far superior in power succeeds in catching me.[20]

Already, even at this early stage, the strain of independent command was beginning to tell on von Spee. Despite his stunning victory, he now became besieged by indecision and a degree of fatalism that moved beyond the pragmatic and left him with the all-encompassing sadness and despair that could, ultimately, have only one outcome. He became curt and sharp in his dealings with the public, sometimes displaying his short temper in surprising ways.

When, after being entertained at the German club one evening, a man suggested drinking a toast to 'the damnation of the English,' von Spee was quick to snap back at him. 'I will drink to an honourable and courageous foe,' he insisted. Quite probably he was thinking about that evening in Hong Kong a year before when he had entertained the officers of the *Monmouth* to dinner.

Von Spee did not know if these were the men who were now lying dead on the bed of the Pacific Ocean or if the *Monmouth* now had a different crew. But he knew that whoever had fought the battle against him, they were brave sailors who deserved to be respected and praised. It was an attitude that many of the deliriously happy German civilians could not understand.

Although in Britain the news of Craddock's defeat was, at first, met with disbelief, this soon changed to anger and hurt pride. Churchill had not, for one second, thought that Craddock would sail without the *Canopus*, even though he had not protested when informed that the old pre-Dreadnought was being relegated to convoy duties. However that might be, now he and Lord Fisher, the new First Sea Lord, began to plan their revenge on von Spee.

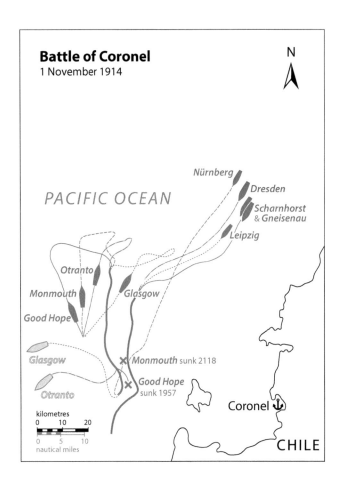

Winston Churchill, First Lord of the Admiralty, and the new First Sea Lord Jacky Fisher outside the Admiralty. Fisher, having replaced Prince Louis of Battenberg a few days before the disaster at Coronel, was immediately faced with the task of how to respond.

Churchill had placed enormous faith in his citadel, the battleship *Canopus*. This later photograph shows the old ship firing her 12 inch guns at the Dardanelles in 1915. It remains a moot point as to whether her presence in the battle line would have made any difference to the outcome at Coronel.

There is no doubt that Kit Craddock had fought a poor action at Coronel where he was out-gunned and out-generalled by von Spee. Yet, given the poor quality of his ships, the result of the battle was never really in doubt. Even if he had taken *Canopus* with him it is unlikely that the outcome would have been very different.

Despite what, at first sight, seemed a clear advantage for the British, the 12 inch guns of the *Canopus* were no match for the 8.2 inch weapons of the *Scharnhorst* and *Gneisenau*—as their later performance against the battle cruisers at the Falklands was to show—and if the three ships had come to blows the *Canopus* would undoubtedly have been out-ranged. With their vastly greater speed the German cruisers could easily have sent the old ship to the bottom as quickly as they did *Good Hope* and *Monmouth*. No, the real strength of the *Canopus* lay simply in her threat.

Von Spee could not afford damage to any of his ships. He had no repair base or dockyard facilities and anything more than superficial harm would have spelled disaster for him. A direct hit from just one of the big shells of the *Canopus* could have caused untold disaster and, therefore, if Craddock had delayed and waited for her to catch him up, it is more than likely that von Spee would have declined to fight. Yet that was not Craddock's way. In the best traditions of the Royal Navy he had hunted down and, with great courage, taken on a vastly superior force. And by doing so, he sealed his fate.

The William Denbow Affair

Perhaps the final—and arguably the greatest—tragedy of the Battle of Coronel came in the shape and person of the Engineer Commander of HMS *Canopus*, William Denbow. For two years Denbow had been on board the *Canopus*, during the time she had been mothballed in Care and Maintenance at Milford. He was the man responsible for maintaining the engines of the old ship, a task he undertook dutifully and diligently. It may have been a lonely posting but Denbow was so efficient in his task that when *Canopus* joined the Third Fleet for the test mobilisation on 18 July 1914, she performed remarkably well. On a three hour trial run she managed to make 17 knots, only 1 knot less than her top speed when she was brand new. Small wonder that Churchill and Battenberg, then First Sea Lord, considered her fit for purpose with Craddock down at the Falkland Islands. Although crewed mainly by Reservists, when the *Canopus* was sent south, Denbow went with her. Lieutenant Start, the ship's senior engineer, was satisfied enough with the performance of her engines but did become increasingly concerned that not once during the cruise south did he see his superior officer, Engineer Commander Denbow. Start may not have seen the man—and all the evidence seems to indicate that Denbow spent almost the entire voyage in his cabin—but Captain Heathcoat Grant certainly did. Denbow told Grant that the old ship could not make more than 12 knots and this was the information that was passed to Craddock. Put quite simply, Commander Denbow was making it up. He was lying although his motives behind this seem unclear. By the time Grant realised the truth Craddock was already away into the Pacific and the captain never passed on the news. Even if he had, it is unlikely that Craddock would have waited. And Denbow? The ship's doctors kept him under observation for some days and finally decided that, mentally, he was in a bad state. He was sent back to Britain on a merchant ship and was invalided out of the service. Later in the war Denbow would have been diagnosed with neurasthenia or some such complaint. In 1914, in the wake of Coronel, his actions were swept quietly under the carpet and no action seems to have been taken against him.

The British Response

When, a few weeks after the declaration of war, Prince Louis of Battenberg tendered his resignation as First Sea Lord it was partly because of the Germanic nature of his background and partly the virulent campaign waged against him in the pages of the popular press. He was German born and still owned estates, where he liked to spend long periods of leisure, in Germany. He spoke with a pronounced German accent and had a brother-in-law who was a High Admiral in the German Navy. He was an efficient peacetime administrator but was not popular. Jacky Fisher once told Churchill that Battenberg had only three friends and two of those were Churchill and himself.

As the war went on Battenberg became increasingly upset and demoralized and was certainly not capable of insightful judgements and the instant decision making that conflict on a world-wide scale now demanded. Those were qualities that his replacement, the new First Sea Lord, had in abundance.

Jacky Fisher had been First Sea Lord before. He was the man behind the Dreadnought programme of the early 1900s and now, when Winston Churchill recalled him from retirement, he brought with him all the dynamism for which he was famous. In many respects a brutal and vicious man, Fisher's appointment was not unanimously popular. The public might love Fisher, the King certainly did not. He distrusted him and it needed the threat of resignation from Churchill—something the government certainly did not want—before Fisher was confirmed in post.

Whatever else Fisher might be, he was certainly energetic and brought to the Admiralty a degree of urgency that had previously been lacking. Within an hour of the news that Craddock had been defeated reaching London, Fisher and Churchill were in conference.

In what was really a tacit acceptance that the addition of *Canopus* to Craddock's Squadron had been far too inadequate a response to the German threat, Churchill now proposed removing a new battle cruiser from the Grand Fleet and, along with the *Defence*, sending her out to deal with von Spee. When he suggested this to Lord Fisher, he was startled at the First Sea Lord's response:–

Admiral Jacky Fisher was a man of strong feelings. Despite his active dislike of Sir Frederick Doveton Sturdee, he agreed to Churchill appointing him to command of the avenging Squadron. Two modern battlecruisers, the *Invincible* and *Inflexible*, were the backbone of his command. This early photograph shows him as a Vice Admiral, and was therefore taken between 1896 and 1901.

I found Lord Fisher in a bolder mood. He would take two battle cruisers from the Grand Fleet for the South American station—he would take a third, the *Princess Royal*, for Halifax and later for the West Indies in case von Spee came through the Panama Canal.[21]

Admiral Jellicoe, commander of the Grand Fleet, rightly protested about the removal of the third battle cruiser from his Fleet, believing that it was an unnecessary move, but made no complaints about the other two. The *Invincible* and *Inflexible* were duly sent to Devonport to take on stores and have their bottoms scraped to ensure maximum possible speed. When the Admiral Superintendent of the dockyard told the Admiralty that he could not have the two ships ready before Friday 13 November, Fisher replied with the curt message that they were to sail on the 11 of the month:–

The unhappy Superintendent dashed up to London to protest but was met by the irascible Fisher who told him simply and rudely 'By the time you get back to your Dockyard the ships will have sailed.'[22]

They had. The ships left on the afternoon of 11 November, without pomp or ceremony and with a strict wireless silence that ensured the Germans, and von Spee in particular, could have no idea what was coming towards them. In the southern seas the two battle cruisers were to rendezvous with four armoured cruisers—the *Defence*, *Cornwall*, *Carnarvon* and *Kent*—two light cruisers, the *Glasgow* and *Bristol*, and the old *Canopus*. It was a force that would have made Kit Craddock lick his lips in anticipation.

Commanding the two battle cruisers and flying his flag in the *Invincible* was the new commander of the powerful South Atlantic and South Pacific Squadron, Admiral Sir Frederick Doveton Sturdee, the former Chief of Staff at the Admiralty.

The defeat at Coronel was, in many respects, the culmination of a mismanaged campaign where Craddock had been denied adequate resources and the ships to fight von Spee. For this Admiral Sturdee, like Winston Churchill and Prince Louis of Battenberg, the First Lord of the Admiralty and First Sea Lord respectively, was partly to blame.

However, to dismiss Sturdee from his post as Chief of Staff, as Fisher wanted to do—they had been implacable enemies for years, Fisher regarding him as a 'pedantic ass'—would have been to set him up as a scapegoat. And Churchill wanted no blame to be attached to any aspect of the Admiralty's practice or conduct of the war thus far.

The war had not begun well for the Royal Navy, the supposed bastion of the British coast. On the opening day of the conflict the cruiser *Amphion* had been mined and sunk in the North Sea, followed soon after by the *Aboukir*, *Hogue* and *Cressey*, all three torpedoed by the same submarine on the same day.

Then came the escape of the *Goeben* and *Breslau* which, in a daring and romantic dash, had managed to avoid the ships of Admiral Milne in the Mediterranean and

The battlecruiser *Inflexible*. Fast, well-armed, she was the ideal ship to help re-take command of the southern seas after Craddock's defeat. Jacky Fisher originally suggested taking three battle cruisers from the Grand Fleet but Jellicoe protested and it was left at just two.

The battlecruiser *Invincible*, seen here at top speed. Clouds of black smoke from her funnels was a major problem during the Battle of the Falkland Islands, causing Admiral Sturdee to turn away and allow range finders to get an accurate sighting of the enemy.

Admiral Frederick Doveton Sturdee, Chief of Staff at the Admiralty under Prince Louis of Battenberg but now restored to sea-going command.

The war had not begun well for Britain. The old cruiser *Aboukir*—seen here, in an artist's impression, sinking after being torpedoed—was quickly followed by the *Hogue* and *Cressey*, all sunk on the same day by the same U-Boat. Then came Coronel—Britain badly needed a victory.

find sanctuary in Turkey. It was an episode that left the British with more than a little egg on their faces and something that was only partially offset by Beatty's success in the minor skirmish at the Heligoland Bight at the end of August. So to incur further blame or discredit for the Admiralty was the last thing Churchill wanted.

Craddock's defeat could—just—be attributed to his own impetuosity and tactical mistakes but if Sturdee was now summarily sacked it would not look good. And yet Churchill knew that Fisher and Sturdee could never work together. Sturdee was asked if he would resign. He refused and then, with his usual political adroitness, Churchill saw a way out of the dilemma—he would appoint Sturdee as the admiral commanding the new force.

Fisher agreed. There was always the danger that victory over von Spee would make Sturdee a national hero but it was, the new First Sea Lord felt, a risk worth taking. The powerful battle cruisers should make short work of the *Scharnhorst* and *Gneisenau* and, at this stage at least, removing von Spee from the equation was more important than any petty jealousies. There is a story that Fisher exclaimed 'Sturdee caused the mess, Sturdee can sort it out.' While being exactly the sort of vitriol the new First Sea Lord might well have uttered, it has little credibility. The new world-wide disposition of British ships, pulling together 30 vessels to defeat von Spee and over seventy more for duties such as convoy protection and chasing the *Emden* and *Königsberg*, was as much Sturdee's work as it was Battenberg's and Churchill's.

As Churchill later wrote, resources were stretched to the maximum, they could not lay hands on another vessel.[23] Popular belief might have said that Fisher threw the plan together on his arrival at the Admiralty. In fact, it was already in existence. All Fisher did was to tweak it a little and then sit back and take the credit.

When he was offered the command, Sturdee, always a sea going man at heart, accepted with alacrity. Having planned the new dispositions just a few weeks before, he was now in a position to implement all the changes that he, Battenberg and Fisher had talked about.

The German Moves

Guessing where von Spee would turn up next was a difficult task. It was something the German admiral did not even know himself. Before Coronel his choices were severely restricted but he now had so many options that were suddenly laid open before him.

He might head for the Indian Ocean where, as von Müller on the *Emden* was demonstrating, the opportunities for raiding were endless. Or he could sail around the Cape of Good Hope to intercept troop convoys on the African coast. He might head north and transit the Panama Canal—opened only a few months before the outbreak of war—and cause havoc in the Caribbean. What to do? What to do?

Von Spee remained undecided for some time. He delayed for nearly two weeks after leaving Valparaiso and arriving at Mas a Fuera where his light cruisers were waiting for him. He even sent *Dresden* and *Leipzig* back to Valparaiso in order to scotch a rumour that they had been sunk at Coronel. It worked but their sudden appearance also told the British that the East Asiatic Squadron was still on the Pacific coast of South America—priceless intelligence. The two cruisers finally left Valparaiso to rejoin the fleet and at last von Spee made his decision. He would head for the Cape and the South Atlantic. On 15 November he sailed south, leaving *Dresden* and *Leipzig* to catch him up—which they did three days later.

On 21 November the German Squadron anchored in St Quentin Bay. It was here that von Spee learned that the Kaiser had awarded him the Iron Cross, First Class, as well as 300 Iron Crosses, Second Class, to be apportioned out to his officers and men. A celebration was clearly in order and giving out the medals took the best part of a full day with von Spee moving by admiral's barge from ship to ship. Ceremony over, it was time to move but, strangely and inexplicably, von Spee chose to remain at St Quentin for a further five days.

In reply to a telegram from the German Admiralty asking about his next course of action, von Spee signalled simply 'The cruiser Squadron intends to break through for home.'[24] His ships took on coal from three colliers that had recently slipped out of Chilean ports and he finally began rounding the Horn only on the 26th of the month.

After the Battle of Coronel the German Squadron sailed to Valparaiso where von Spee and his ships received a welcome reserved for heroes. They had suffered no damage during the battle.

In delaying his voyage around the Horn Admiral von Spee had made what was to prove a costly tactical mistake. Bad weather off the Cape—storms so severe that the squadron could make no more than 5 knots—delayed them further, forcing the light cruisers to jettison valuable coal from their decks and it was not until 1 December that they finally managed to sail around the southernmost point of South America. Despite the appalling weather they were around the Cape, almost in the Atlantic, and despite all the delays and prevarication, the mood in the squadron was buoyant.

6

Hunting the Emden—
The Cruise Begins

When, in August 1914, the light cruiser *Emden* parted from Admiral von Spee and the rest of the East Asiatic Squadron, to operate as a lone raider in the Indian Ocean, Captain Karl von Müller signalled briefly to the flagship:–

> I thank Your Excellency for the confidence placed in me. I wish the Cruiser Squadron a successful cruise.[25]

Despite his good wishes, von Müller did not have much faith in the long-term prospects for von Spee's Squadron—or, for that matter, his own. Von Spee's Squadron would, he thought, be inactive for many weeks, cruising aimlessly in the Pacific. It would certainly meet disaster if brought to action by a superior force.

A lone raider, on the other hand, might have more success, even if the end result was bound to be death and disaster. Von Müller knew that the cruise on which he was embarking was a desperate mission. He would hunt down enemy merchant shipping, depriving Britain and her Allies of essential raw materials and provisions. He would disrupt trade and, hopefully, cause panic in the enemy ranks. But he knew that if it came to a fight with enemy warships there could, ultimately, be only one result. His time was limited but until he was caught he would operate to the best of his ability.

Von Müller was, in many respects, a perfect Prussian officer and gentleman. Tall, blond and precise in his thoughts and actions, he was the son of a Prussian Colonel and the ideal man to lead a lone hunting campaign. He had been captain of the *Emden* for nearly twenty-four months and, in a strange, almost mystical way, relished the loneliness of command. He was shy but knew his own inner strengths and was able to make his decisions, on the surface at least, without any of the self-doubt that might have plagued other cruiser captains of the time.

Karl von Müller was, perhaps, not as loved as von Spee, his shyness making him distant and self-contained. He could be reckless when the mood took him but such recklessness was invariably backed up by cool judgement and by the workings of a perfect analytical brain. He had a degree of arrogance and pride

Above: The light cruiser *Emden*, fast, beautiful to look at and the ideal vessel to wage a lonely, piratical war.

Right: A wooden effigy of Captain Karl von Müller of the *Emden*. Such was his popularity back home in Germany that citizens of the city of Emden happily paid a few pennies to knock nails into the wooden statue of the man, all the proceeds going to war charities.

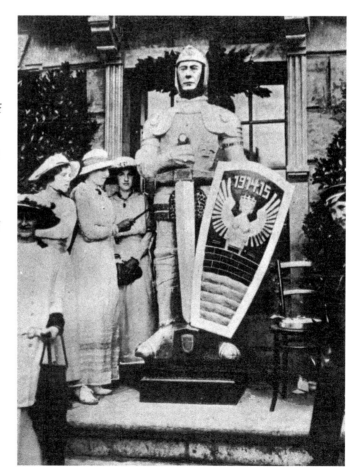

in his own ability and was not afraid to admit that this was the type of operation for which he had always been intended.

The *Emden*'s crew, all 320 of them, had been moulded by von Müller into an effective and efficient fighting team. Each man knew his job and was confident in his ability to carry out any orders he might be given. Initiative was encouraged by von Müller and the crew of the *Emden* knew that they were the crème de la crème of the German Navy.

The officers were a particularly interesting assortment of characters. Prinz von Hohenzollern was from one of the great noble families of Germany, a man with an intellect to match that of his captain, while Lieutenant Lauterbach and Lieutenant-Commander Hellmuth von Mücke, the latter being *Emden*'s First Lieutenant, were both powerful individuals who could be counted on to do their duty to their final breath.

The ship itself was not the newest German cruiser, having been completed as far back as 1908, but she was fast and pristine, her crew being rightly proud of her appearance. 'The Swan of the East,' they called her—and rightly so as she was a beautiful little ship with teak decks and a compact graceful line. She was armed with ten 4.1 inch guns, each with a range of over 10,000 yards, more than enough to deal with merchant ships but probably not heavy enough if faced by the heavy weapons of an armoured cruiser like the *Defence* or *Hampshire*. She was also equipped with two 17 inch torpedo tubes.

Early Successes

The *Emden*, accompanied by the supply ship *Marcomannia*, left Pagan Island on 14 August, just two days after von Spee had sailed away. They headed west, coaling at Timor before cruising on across the Indian Ocean.

Von Müller was already planning his campaign. He quickly had his ship's carpenters hard at work, disguising the *Emden* with an extra dummy funnel. Von Müller's thinking was that with the addition of a fourth funnel his ship would look just like the British cruiser *Yarmouth*,—the 'bloody *Yarmouth*' as one signal from the *Marcomannia* read. It was a ruse that, right to the end, certainly seemed to work.

Luck was with the German ship. At the beginning of September von Müller took her into a deserted bay to the east of Simalur Island in order to coal, an anchorage that had been visited and searched by the cruiser *Hampshire* just twenty four hours before. And then her career as a raider really began. Hellmuth von Muüke later wrote about the activities of the ship:–

> By the beginning of September, 1914, we reached the Bay of Bengal, on the look-out for prey on the trade routes. On the 11th a large steamer was sighted ahead. Assuming we were a British man-of-war she at once hoisted a large British flag to signify her joy at our presence. I regret I did not see the foolish face of her skipper when we hoisted our ensign and politely signalled her to join us.[26]

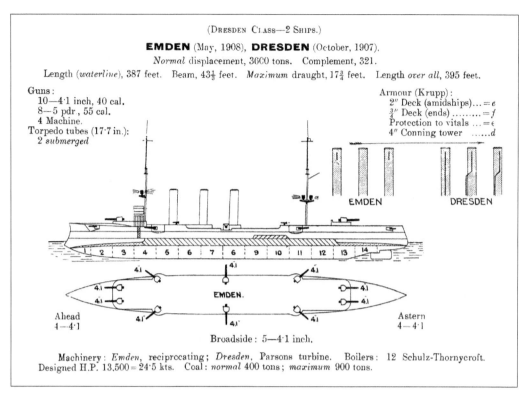

(DRESDEN CLASS—2 SHIPS.)

EMDEN (May, 1908), **DRESDEN** (October, 1907).

Normal displacement, 3600 tons. Complement, 321.

Length (*waterline*), 387 feet. Beam, 43⅓ feet. *Maximum* draught, 17¾ feet. Length *over all*, 395 feet.

Guns :
  10—4·1 inch, 40 cal.
  8—5 pdr , 55 cal.
  4 Machine.
Torpedo tubes (17·7 in.):
  2 *submerged*

Armour (Krupp):
  2″ Deck (amidships)... $= e$
  ¾″ Deck (ends) .... $= f$
  Protection to vitals ... $= \epsilon$
  4″ Conning tower ......d

EMDEN   DRESDEN

EMDEN.

Ahead
4—4·1

Astern
4—4·1

Broadside : 5—4·1 inch.

Machinery : *Emden*, reciprocating ; *Dresden*, Parsons turbine. Boilers : 12 Schulz-Thornycroft. Designed H.P. 13,500 = 24·5 kts. Coal : *normal* 400 tons ; *maximum* 900 tons.

A contemporary plan from *Jane's All the World's Fighting Ships*.

A wartime convoy under way. Such was the fear of the *Emden*'s activities that New Zealand and Australia suspended troop convoys until the raider was captured.

That first prize yielded a huge supply of soap, enough to keep the crew of the *Emden* clean for at least a year. Like many of the other victims of the raider, this prize vessel was kept as a prison or, as Mücke called it, a 'rogues depot,' until she was full and then sent on her way—minus, of course, all of her valuable cargo.

The dummy funnel was an ingenuous device and certainly helped the *Emden* to approach unsuspecting merchant ships but the use of wireless—von Müller and his officers using the strength of in-coming signals to work out distance and type of vessel approaching—enabled her to stay well clear of enemy warships. Von Mücke again:–

> Our business flourished; as soon as a steamer came our way she was stopped and one officer and, say, ten men were sent aboard and made her ready to be sunk. Another masthead generally appeared on the horizon. There was no need to hurry; they simply came our way. At times we had five or six vessels collected on one spot.[27]

Once, off the coast of Sumatra, the *Emden* came within touching distance of the *Hampshire* which was leading the hunt for her. The British never knew how close they came. Hugging the shore, von Müller watched the British ship steam past, outlined against the night sky, then took his ship into harbour to coal once more from the *Marcomannia*.

Merchant ships began to fall with increasing regularity into von Müller's hands. Five, ten, a dozen prizes, the count was steadily rising, and before long the *Emden* was so successful that the Admiralty was forced to order all vessels trading

In a few short weeks the *Emden* had sunk over twenty merchant ships. Thanks to the gentlemanly conduct of von Müller and his crew there were few casualties, sailors being allowed to abandon ship before their vessel was sunk or taken into captivity.

in the Bay of Bengal to remain in port. When all trade between Colombo and Singapore was halted, von Müller knew he had achieved one of his major aims.

Headlines all over the world began to scream about the success of this single German raider. Prices on the Stock Exchange plummeted and, to the chagrin of Field Marshal Kitchener, British Minister for War, and the War Office, the New Zealand government refused to dispatch a convoy of ANZAC troops from Wellington. The troops were urgently needed to fill gaps on the Western Front. Now they were sitting, twiddling their thumbs in port while the war in France raged on. The New Zealand attitude was understandable. The convoy was supposed to be guarded by three antiquated cruisers, vessels so old that they had no hope of ever getting close to the *Emden*. As long as the *Emden*—as well as von Spee—were loose in the southern oceans the threat to this and future convoys was a real, live one.

New Tactics

Despite his success Karl von Müller had grown tired of commerce raiding. There was little challenge in stopping and sinking unarmed merchantmen. He wanted something that was more daring and which would provide Germany with a major propaganda scoop.

Despite being closely chased by Captain Grant in the cruiser *Hampshire*, von Müller decided upon a new course of action, one which was dangerous for his ship but which, if everything turned out well, would bring him and Germany enormous kudos.

On 22 September von Müller conned his ship through the sandbanks outside Madras on the Indian coast. He edged past the lighthouse and hove to, close in to shore, where the oil tanks of the Burmah Oil Company lay waiting. There were shore defences including six large howitzers and a battery of 15 pounders but several of these guns had to be brought into action on bullock carts, and before the defenders even knew what was happening, the *Emden*'s searchlights blazed on. The blinding lights were followed by salvo after salvo of four inch shells. Hellmuth von Mülke later wrote:–

> Arriving off Madras we test the oil tanks. Only the previous day the official news of our end had been announced—We advanced up to 3,000 metres, the lighthouse, peacefully aglow, facilitating navigation. A few shots, then a heavy black cloud. We had expedited several million worth into the air.[28]

The *Emden*'s wireless then picked up signals from the hunting *Hampshire*, close behind, and the German raider slipped away before the British ship could arrive on the scene. When *Hampshire* followed the *Emden* into the harbour at Madras she found only blazing oil tanks and a population in chaos after the terror that a sudden and unexpected night attack from the sea was bound to bring.

Von Müller did think of trying the same trick at Colombo but searchlights sweeping through the night sky warned him off. Instead he sank several more merchantmen and public panic rose to epidemic proportions. Insurance rates shot through the roof.

However, von Müller knew that his men could not continue without a period of rest and recuperation. They needed fresh food and a change from the monotonous round of waiting followed by quick action and then still more waiting. Just as importantly, his ship needed to be overhauled after several months hard effort.

Consequently, the *Emden* slipped away from the Indian coast and found refuge on the remote and charming island of Diego Garcia—where the crew encountered an aged local who had no idea that Britain and Germany were at loggerheads. They kept him full of whiskey and when the *Emden* eventually sailed away he still had no idea that the rest of the world was at war.

The Sinking of the Zhemchug

There was some success for the hunters when, on 6 October, the *Marcomannia* was caught and sunk by the *Yarmouth*, leaving the *Emden* without a supply ship. Nevertheless, von Müller sank his twenty-first victim soon afterwards, the

An unusual postcard view showing one of the *Emden*'s light guns on display in Australia after the raider had been sunk.

collier *Exford*. Capturing the Admiralty collier brought the *Emden* yet another full hold of best Welsh coal.

Von Müller now began to plan a new operation. The German port or colony of Tsingtao had, as von Spee expected, been besieged by Japanese forces since the middle of September. It was isolated and of little tactical or strategic use in a war like this but the defenders clung on, refusing to surrender. With the battleship *Triumph* included in what was, essentially, a Japanese operation the port was bombarded while Japanese soldiers invested the town from the landward side. By early October it was clear that Tsingtao was likely to fall any day and von Müller decided that he needed to do something to compensate for what was clearly going to be a loss in German prestige.

Penang was the most important British port between Calcutta and Singapore and this was the target von Müller had in mind. Hellmuth von Mücke was on the *Emden*'s bridge for the whole operation:–

On the morning of October 28th, whilst it was still dark, we were making the port at twenty knots—As we approached the inner roadstead the sun was just on the point of rising. We could see, in the twilight, quite a number of steamers; but no sign of a warship.[29]

Von Mücke, with a bravado that runs right the way through his account of the *Emden*'s career, claimed that they were hoping to encounter and fight a warship. Although his captain was determined to make a big show, this was unlikely. Just as with von Spee, the *Emden*'s captain knew he could not afford damage to his ship. Destruction of dock facilities and merchantmen was the more likely aim.

They may not have been looking for a warship but in the early morning light that was exactly what they found:–

In the midst of the trading vessels a black mass appeared; not until we had approached to within 250 metres did we know with certainty that she was the Russian *Zhemchug*. On board her everyone was sleeping. We first fired a torpedo which hit the stern. There was activity on board; we could see a number of Russian officers rushing on deck and throwing themselves into the water. Our guns shelled the forepart of the *Zhemchug* with such a hail of projectiles that after a few minutes it looked like a sieve. The fires below could be plainly seen through the holes.[30]

The battle—if it can be called that—did not last long. Two of the Russian guns managed to open fire but then a second torpedo from the *Emden* slammed into the side of the *Zhemchug* and there was a huge explosion as her magazine detonated. The shock waves threw sailors on the *Emden* off their feet and rocked the ship from side to side. When the smoke cleared the *Zhemchug* had totally disappeared.

As sampans came flocking out of Penang to pick up survivors, the *Emden* turned for the harbour mouth. She stopped to capture the steamer *Glenturret* which, unsuspecting, was about to enter port but was then challenged by the French torpedo boat destroyer *Mousquet*. As von Mücke later commented:–

> She steamed towards us at fifteen knots as if nothing had happened. Our fourth funnel was still up and we had no flag hoisted. At 4,000 metres we opened fire and several minutes later there was nothing to be seen of her. Even after the third salvo she must have been reduced to a heap of fragments. She had accepted action, fired at us with guns and torpedoes, but without success.[31]

With the battle won, the *Emden* lowered her boats to pick up survivors. Thirty three of them were pulled from the water and, humanely, later passed on to a British steamer they encountered on their travels.

Daylight had now come and the *Emden* headed for open water. Two French gunboats, the *Fronde* and *Pistolet*, gave chase for a while but the German raider soon showed them a clean pair of heels and disappeared over the horizon. The poor captain of the *Zhemchug* survived the disaster only to be court martialled and reduced to the ranks as an ordinary seaman for his part in a pretty sorry skirmish.

Arguably, the action at Penang saw von Müller at the height of his fame and success. He had acted with bravery and courtesy and, aided by incredible good fortune, had managed to avoid all of the ships that were looking for him. But

Zhemchug was the second of the two-vessel Izumrud class of protected cruisers built for the Imperial Russian Navy and launched in 1901. *Emden*'s second torpedo broke the ship in two; the explosion killed 89 crewmen, and wounded 143 others and the ship quickly sank.

The wreck of SMS *Emden* from a photograph taken by an officer from the former Canadian Pacific liner *Empress of Japan*, later an armed merchant cruiser in the service of the Royal Navy.

now, as he steamed for the Sunda Strait, away from Penang, more and more vessels were being deployed against him.

The Japanese sent three cruisers and the *Gloucester* was immediately detached from the Mediterranean Squadron. With the campaign in East Africa—for the moment at least—seeming to be going well, Winston Churchill at the Admiralty felt confident in sending the *Dartmouth* and *Weymouth* to join the hunters.

The ANZAC convoy had at last left Wellington, escorted now by fast modern warships like the *Sydney* and the Japanese *Ibuki*. Von Müller did not know it but the jaws of the trap were beginning to close on the *Emden*.

The End of the Adventure

By the beginning of November 1914 Captain Karl von Müller had been at large for well over two months. He and his ship had sailed over 30,000 nautical miles and had captured or sunk 23 merchantmen, sending their valuable cargoes to the bottom or, if those cargoes were coal, adding them to the boilers and storeroom of the *Emden*. In addition they had destroyed one Russian cruiser and one French destroyer and caused untold damage to the British oil instillations at Madras. Von Müller's plan, now, was to attack and destroy the cable and wireless station on the Cocos Islands. Cutting the cables to Australia would undoubtedly cause yet more panic, he thought, and he knew that he had to keep his crew active:–

Inertia at this stage represented the greatest danger. His ship was typical of this: no longer the 'Swan of the East,' but a filthy hulk, smelling of pigs and pigeons.[32]

Early on the morning of 9 November, the *Emden* arrived off Keeling Island in the Cocos Island group. Lieutenant Commander von Mücke and forty nine men were sent ashore to destroy the instillations. Unfortunately for the Germans, Darcy Farrant, the Superintendent of the WT station recognised the *Emden*'s fourth funnel for what it was, a dummy. Despite the German's attempt at blocking any signals from the station, Farrant managed to get a message away before von Mücke arrived, telling the world that a strange vessel and boatloads of armed men were approaching Keeling Island. The signal was picked up by the ANZAC convoy, now barely fifty miles away and the Australian light cruiser *Sydney* under Captain John Glossop was immediately detached to investigate.

On Keeling Island, von Mücke had almost finished his destruction work. It had taken him and his men the best part of two and a half hours:–

> Then suddenly the *Emden* blew her siren. This was the signal to hasten back with all speed—As I pushed off I saw that the *Emden* had already weighed and was leaving the harbour. First of all I steamed as fast as my pinnace would go, because I had no idea what her intentions were. I thought she was going to meet our coaling ship, as it was intended to coal that day. Suddenly she opened fire.[33]

The *Emden* had been surprised, von Müller's sixth sense finally failing him. Glossop on the *Sydney* was overjoyed at finding the elusive *Emden* and immediately cleared for action. Although *Sydney* was faster than the German ship, the two cruisers were otherwise fairly evenly matched, the German 4.1 inch guns reaching just as far as Sydney's eight 6 inch weapons. And to begin with the *Emden* was both fast and accurate in her firing. With just the second salvo the *Sydney*'s range finder was hit and destroyed and fire broke out in the Australian ship's after control station.

With von Müller desperately trying to close the range, Glossop used his superior speed to stay out of harm's way. Then he suddenly turned to port and opened fire again. Soon salvo after salvo was hitting the German raider.

Realising he could do nothing to help his colleagues, von Mücke and his party had, by now, returned to the island and from there they watched the sad ending of their ship:–

> The shots of the enemy took great effect against the unarmoured portion of the *Emden*. In about a quarter of an hour one of *Emden*'s funnels had already gone and she was burning fiercely aft. Then she made for the enemy at full speed to fire a torpedo, whereby she lost her foremast.[34]

The torpedo missed its mark and Glossop soon realised that his gunfire was having a telling effect on the *Emden*. First one of the German guns fell silent, then another. The *Emden*'s firing wavered, then grew inaccurate, as the casualties

The landing party from the *Emden* under the command of Lieutenant Commander von Mücke.

It was inevitable that, sooner or later, the *Emden*'s luck would run out. This shows the battered ship on the reef at Keeling Island after she had been run to earth and destroyed by the *Sydney*.

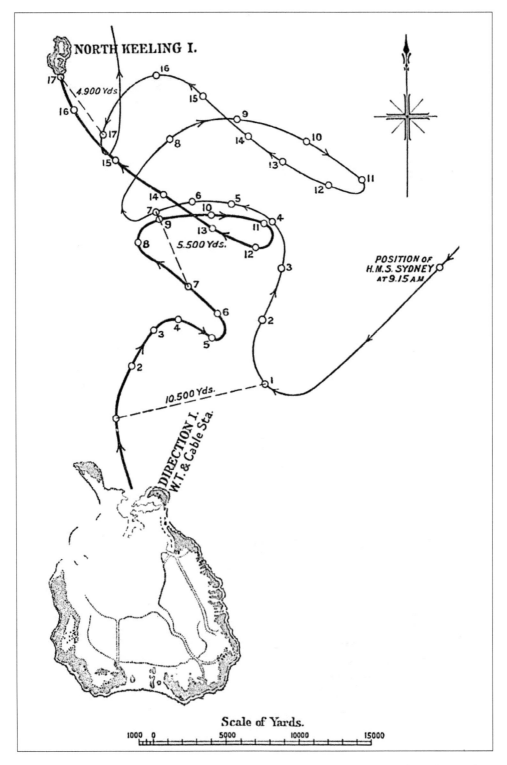

The thin line is the course of HMAS *Sydney*, the thick line that of SMS *Emden*. The numbers indicate the relative positions of the two vessels during the action. Direction Island Wireless Telegraphy Station was at latitude 12° 5½′S, longitude 96° 53½′E (approx).

The Australian cruiser *Sydney*, under Captain Glossop, eventually surprised the *Emden* as she was attempting to cut the telegraph cables at Keeling Island. Despite some initial success, the *Emden* was no match for the larger, better armed *Sydney*.

HMAS *Sydney* was a *Chatham* class light cruiser of the Royal Australian Navy. Launched in 1912, the cruiser was commissioned into the RAN in 1913. During the early stages of the War *Sydney* was involved in supporting the Australian Naval and Military Expeditionary Force, and escorting the first ANZAC convoy. On 9 November 1914, the cruiser defeated SMS *Emden* at the Cocos Islands.

mounted. The navigating officer was blown to pieces, the gunnery officer mortally wounded and, finally, just after 11.00 the ship's third funnel was blown away.

Von Müller was desperate to avoid capture. If he could not sail her any more he would ensure that the *Emden* would be no use to the Allies, either. Using her final burst of steam, he drove the *Emden* towards the rocks of Keeling Island. Glossop tried to stop her, pouring round after round into the battered raider. Doomed but determined, the *Emden* smashed into the rocks of North Keeling Island, ripping thirty feet out of her hull and jamming herself onto the reef.

Silence descended as the *Sydney* turned away and set off to hunt down the *Emden*'s last remaining collier, a former British steam ship that had approached Keeling Island during the battle. This was quickly achieved and late in the afternoon the Australian ship came back to the island.

By now Prinz Hohenzollern and others had got the wounded out from below decks. They lay within sight of the shore, parched with thirst, trying to ward off the gulls that came scavenging down, pecking at the blood and open wounds on their faces. 'Will you surrender?' signalled Glossop. There was no response as the Germans had no signal books on board and with the German ensign still flying Glossop had no option but to open fire again.

As more salvos fell on his ship von Müller himself ran up a white flag and then burned the German ensign. When daylight came the following morning, Captain Glossop came on board the battered *Emden* where von Müller formally presented him with his ceremonial sword. Glossop accepted the sword, then, as a token of his respect, promptly returned it to the German.

And Afterwards

Following the destruction of the *Emden* Captain von Müller, along with most of his crew, passed into captivity. Awarded the Iron Cross, First Class, by the Kaiser, he spent the rest of the war in Malta but did not survive the Armistice and Germany's defeat for long. His spirit had been broken by the Kaiser's abdication and by the virtual destruction of the German Navy, to which he had pledged his life, by the victorious Allied powers.

He was elected to the State Parliament of Brunswick but his health was in a poor way. Repeated bouts of malaria took their toll and in the wake of the revolutionary chaos that consumed post-war Germany Karl von Müller retired to the village of Blankenberg. There, a few years later, on 11 March 1923, he died peacefully in his sleep.

Von Müller received world-wide acclaim for his efforts. Even the British press poured praise upon him, lauding his courage and chivalry:–

> It is almost in our heart to regret that the *Emden* has been destroyed. Von Müller has been enterprising, cool and daring in making war on our shipping, and has revealed a nice sense of humour. He has, moreover, shown every possible consideration to

The *Sydney*'s boat takes off prisoners from the *Emden*. Many of the German crew died in the action, many more suffered from attacks by the sea birds that came swooping down, attracted by the blood and open wounds.

SMS *Emden* as a wreck on the reef.

The SMS *Emden* as a wreck on the rocks of Keeling Island.

The SMS *Emden*, beached on the rocks of Keeling Island, Cocos Islands, as viewed from the sea.

the crews of his prizes. There is not a survivor who does not speak well of this young German officer, the officers under him and the crew obedient to his orders.[35]

The *Emden*'s final battle had cost her 133 men killed and many more injured. The wreck, surprisingly, managed to survive the battering of the waves and lay on the reef at Keeling Island for another forty years. It was only finally broken up in the early 1950s. But what of the landing party under Lieutenant Commander Mücke?

Von Mücke may not have been the easiest or friendliest of people but he was a fine sailor. Seeing the end of the *Emden* he immediately took over an old schooner, the *Ayesha* which was lying in the harbour at Keeling Island. Then, under the German ensign, he and his 'crew' set off.

The *Ayesha* was old and her bottom rotten—she had been lying in the bay for over two years. Interestingly, the islanders—including the British workers at the WT station—were far more friendly once the *Emden* had been destroyed. They helped supply the *Ayesha*, warned von Mücke about trying to sail far in such a damaged and dilapidated vessel and then, when they saw he was in earnest, waved him off on his travels.

Despite the dire condition of the old sailing boat, von Mücke and his sailors managed to reach Padang where she was provisioned and remained for a few days. As von Mücke, in his usual haughty style, later wrote:–

> I kept to a northerly course to get to Padang, and we arrived all, more or less, in our birthday costumes.—Here at last we got German papers, old but welcome as we had so far seen only English ones, which gave the usual lying news: Russians near Berlin, Kaiser wounded, Crown Prince killed, epidemic among German generals, revolution etc.[36]

Then they set out again. Two days out from port they ran into the *Choising*, a British steam ship that had been captured by the *Emden* and was now being used as a German collier. Transferring to this ship, the *Ayesha* was scuttled and von Mücke headed for the Yemen. There he chartered a dhow—a second attempt as the first one sank just off shore—and the party finally reached Aqueba.

Travelling now by camel, the German sailors set off across the desert. They lost six men in the constant series of skirmishes that took place with the local Bedouins but finally, in May 1915 they reached Constantinople. It had been an amazing and perilous journey, something of which Captain von Müller himself would have certainly approved.

Lieutenant Lauterbach had an equally strange conclusion to the *Emden* voyage. On 7 November von Müller had sent him in command of the supply ship *Exford* to establish a base and wait for him at Socotra on the coast of mainland Africa.

Unfortunately, before she could reach Africa, the *Exford* was captured by the armed merchant cruiser *Empress of Japan* and Lauterbach was sent to a prisoner of war camp in Singapore. He made several attempts to escape, all unsuccessful, but did finally succeed in starting a mutiny by the guarding Indian soldiers. While the riot was going on, Lauterbach managed to ease out of the camp gate and disappear into the crowd.

He left Singapore hiding in the hold of a sampan with the price of ten thousand pounds on his head. He nearly died in the jungles of Sumatra before, posing as South African Boer, he was hidden by an English girl in Shanghai. He became an American sailor to work his passage to the USA and managed to give prowling British secret service agents the slip in New York. He shipped out of America on a Danish boat to Oslo and in October 1915, a year after the *Emden* was sunk, he finally reached home.[37]

The *Emden* had led a brief but eventful life. She was, in many respects, the ideal 'modern day pirate,' a vessel that had caused mayhem in the Indian Ocean and achieved everything Admiral von Spee and Captain von Müller could ever have hoped for. Hers had been a glorious and romantic adventure that had inspired people from all nations, all walks of life. But she had been just one ship, a single raider. And for the men at the British Admiralty von Spee's victorious squadron was an altogether different problem.

After the battle with HMAS *Sydney* the survivors from the SMS *Emden* and the SS *Buresk* were transported to Colombo on HMAS *Sydney* and SS *Empress of Russia*. Many of the crew were sent onwards to Australia as prisoners of war. This photograph of some of crew was taken during their captivity.

Karl Friedrich Max von Müller, (1873–1923) was Captain of SMS *Emden*. At the outbreak of War *Emden* was anchored at Tsingtao. She departed in the evening of 31 July 1914. On 4 August she intercepted and captured the Russian mail steamer *Rjäsan*, the first prize taken by the Kaiserliche Marine. *Emden* then rendezvoused with the German East Asia Squadron of Admiral-Graf Maximilian von Spee in the Mariana Islands.

It was during a conference at the island of Pagan that Müller proposed a single light cruiser of the squadron be detached to raid Allied commerce in the Indian Ocean, while the remainder of von Spee's Squadron continued east across the Pacific. Kapitän von Müller and *Emden* were given the assignment. In the following 12 weeks the *Emden* and Müller achieved a reputation for daring and chivalry. While taking fourteen prizes, the only merchant sailors killed by the *Emden's* guns were five victims of a shore bombardment of British oil tanks at the port of Madras. *Emden* also sank the Russian cruiser *Zhemchug* and the French destroyer *Mousquet* during a raid on Penang, Malaya. *Emden* was finally cornered by the Australian light cruiser HMAS *Sydney*, and was defeated by its heavier guns.

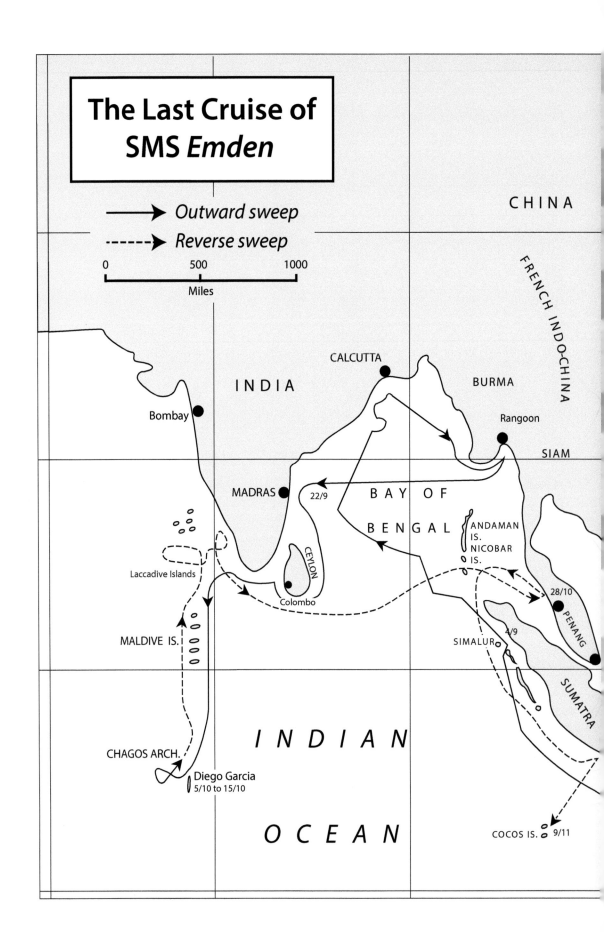

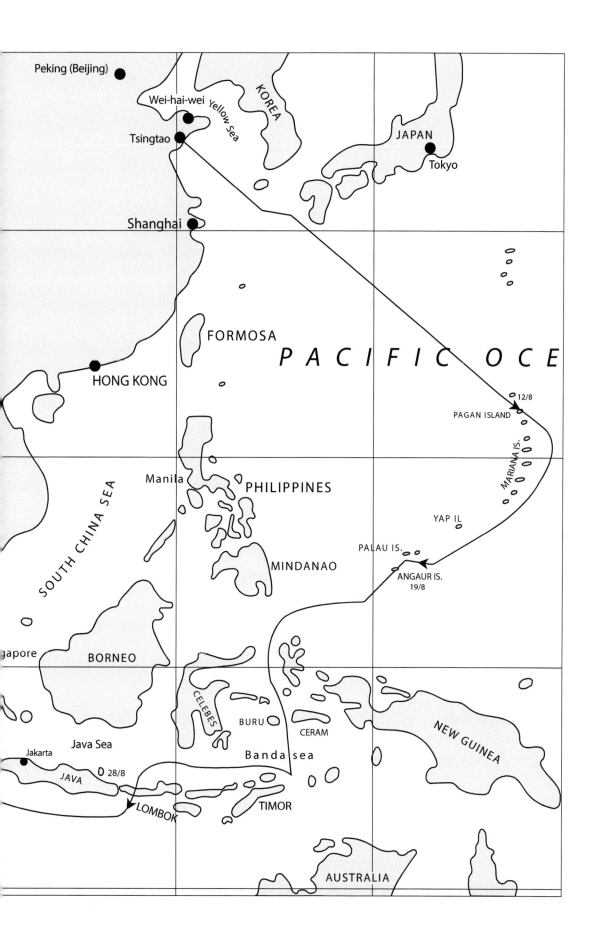

7

Revenge—Heading South

Admiral Sturdee and his two battle cruisers had left Plymouth at dusk on 11 November, a little less than two weeks after the disaster at Coronel. It had been an amazing turn around, the rapidity of fitting out and equipping the ships astounding everyone apart from Churchill and Fisher. But British pride had been damaged and the gathering of Sturdee's new fleet, particularly the two battle cruisers, was as much a 'knee jerk' reaction as it was a considered naval response.

There were no bands, no celebrations as *Invincible* and *Inflexible* steamed out of port and the only spectators—apart from the dockyard workers, who had seen it all before—were the admiral's wife and daughter. Sturdee's course was due south, to a rendezvous with Admiral Stoddart at the Albrohos Rocks off the coast of Brazil.

Waiting for Sturdee at Albrohos were the cruisers *Bristol*, *Carnarvon*, *Cornwall* and *Kent* along with the armed merchant cruisers *Orama* and *Macedonia*. The *Glasgow*, repaired after her mauling at Coronel, was also there, her Captain John Luce eager for another crack at von Spee's Squadron. Admiral Stoddart in the *Defence* also soon arrived.

Despite the speed with which the British fleet had been assembled and dispatched, Sturdee's progress south was, to say the least, leisurely. The accidental death of a Boy Telegraphist on the *Inflexible*, killed in the drum of one of the ship's motors, led to the loss of a complete day as arrangements for his burial at sea were worked out. The young lad finally laid to rest, the voyage continued but still Sturdee seemed in no hurry. In the end:–

> He took twenty-six days. On at least two days the battle cruisers towed targets for each other to practise gunnery. *Invincible* managed to foul one of her propellers with the towing wire, and had to stop for twelve hours to put divers over the side to clear it.[38]

On 21 November the two ships passed over the Equator and the 'crossing the line ceremony' delayed them by a further day. Making a comfortable and economical 10 knots, they eventually reached St Vincente in the Cape Verde

HMS *Inflexible* in more peaceful times. A fine photograph taken in New York City in 1909. HMS *Inflexible* was an *Invincible* class battle cruiser launched in 1907 and commissioned October 1908. After the Battle of the Falklands *Inflexible* bombarded Turkish forts in the Dardanelles in 1915, but was damaged by return fire and struck a mine while manoeuvring. She had to be beached to prevent her from sinking, but she was temporarily repaired and sent to Malta, and then Gibraltar for more permanent repairs. She damaged the German battle cruiser *Lützow* during the Battle of Jutland. She was deemed obsolete after the war and scrapped in 1921.

The *Inflexible, en route* to the Falkland Islands.

At Albrohos Rocks, off the coast of Brazil, Sturdee and his two battle cruisers were met by the rest of his newly formed fleet. The Town Class light cruiser *Caernarvon* was one of these.

The *Bristol*, another ship waiting to greet Sturdee, was already suffering from an engine defect. It did not prevent her joining the squadron but it limited her part in the coming battle to chasing and destroying the German colliers.

HMS *Bristol* was a Town-class light cruiser of the Royal Navy launched in February 1910 and commissioned in December of the same year. On the outbreak of War, she was in the West Indies and was the first British ship to see action, engaging the German raider SMS *Karlsruhe* on 6 August 1914, but *Karlsruhe* used her superior speed to escape.

Admiral Sturdee was an implacable, careful man, the very opposite to the impetuous Kit Craddock. This newspaper photograph of Sturdee, published after the battle, shows him with a slightly mystified look on his face, as if he can barely understand what all the fuss is about.

Islands where the rumour of a German raider in the vicinity delayed them even more. Finally, on 26 November the two battle cruisers reached the Albrohos Rocks to join with the assembled cruisers of Sturdee's new force.

The reasons for Sturdee's calm and sedate progress have never been made clear. He had no fear of von Spee's squadron, out-gunning the Germans in almost all respects. Perhaps he was wary of making the same mistake as Kit Craddock and rushing into things when a little more patience would have been the right course of action. Sturdee was as pragmatic and as careful as Craddock was impulsive. He knew what Fisher thought of him, knew his career was balanced on a knife edge. He would have to tread carefully, taking his time, ensuring that he did not expose himself to sudden attack from a mercurial and tactical wizard like Admiral von Spee. There is no record of his thought processes at this time and it remains, unfortunately, mere supposition.

Whatever the reason for the delay, the first half of his journey was over and his fleet was now assembled. Having arrived at Albrohos Rocks, Sturdee immediately called a conference with Admiral Stoddart and the various cruiser captains where he calmly announced that he would wait for an approaching supply ship and stay three days at Albrohos.

To John Luce of the *Glasgow*, the only ship in the fleet that had actually been involved in combat with von Spee's Squadron, it was a foolish, not to say potentially disastrous, decision. Later, sitting in his cabin on the *Glasgow*, Luce was acutely aware of the dangers of delay. He knew that the British force had to reach the Falkland Islands before von Spee and so, defying years of training and British naval tradition, he felt obliged to return to the flagship and challenge the admiral's decision.

It was a heated discussion but, to Luce's intense satisfaction, Sturdee relented and agreed to change his plans. They would not wait for the supply ship but sail in the morning. Leaving Stoddart to fly his flag in *Defence* and cover his rear by patrolling around the Cape of *Good Hope*, Sturdee ordered his ships to weigh anchor and, once more, they began to head south.

In a line stretching out for 70 miles the two battle cruisers, the five cruisers, the armed merchant cruisers, and their accompanying supply ships—their speed now greatly increased—swept onwards towards Port Stanley in the Falkland Islands. On one day the battle cruisers practiced long distance firing but now, with the threat of action drawing ever closer, they did not lessen their pace.

The fleet eventually made landfall in the Falkland Islands on 7 December when the rugged hills and snow-capped mountains of Britain's southernmost colony finally came into view. Pushing through the hastily created boom defence of the harbour, they anchored and began coaling, either in Port Stanley itself or in Port William, a large anchorage just to the north.

On arrival Sturdee's ships were greeted by the sight of the old *Canopus*, now carefully camouflaged and which, in compliance with Admiralty orders, had run herself up onto the mud in order to cover the harbour entrance.

It was probably the best possible use of the old battleship as her slow

HMS *Glasgow* was commanded in both battles by John Luce. Having already fought von Spee, Luce knew that the British force had to reach the Falkland Islands as quickly as possible and it was down to his argument that Sturdee decided to push on rather than wait at Albrohos Rocks for a few days—luckily as it turned out as the British fleet arrived just a few hours before the Germans.

The rugged terrain of the Falkland Islands is shown here in a photograph taken a few years before war broke out.

speed—her engines having been irrevocably damaged in her recent activities—would have been more of a hindrance than a help if von Spee did come. And moored in a static position her 12 inch guns could fire over a low promontory of land and cover all approaches to the port.

The relief in the tiny community at the arrival of Sturdee's fleet was palpable. The *Canopus* had unloaded her 12 pounder guns and established batteries around the town—even creating a defensive boom of oil filled barrels across the harbour mouth—but everybody, from the Governor to the local postman, knew that would not be enough to defend the colony against the German cruisers. There was no sign of von Spee and several of the newly arrived naval officers quietly began to doubt if he would come at all. Surely if the Falklands was his target he would have been here by now, they thought.

Once coaling was over, everyone knew they would have to begin the hunt for the German Squadron. Sturdee had already made his decision. After two or three days coaling and re-supplying his ships, the fleet would head up the western coast of Chile, more or less following in the footsteps of the luckless Kit Craddock. It would be a long and arduous search.

But, in the meantime, for the officers at least, there might be sufficient time for a few days ashore. The delights of Port Stanley were few enough—a little shooting or fishing, perhaps—but after several weeks at sea any diversion would have been welcome.

Von Spee Arrives

In fact von Spee was closer than anyone could imagine. Strict wireless silence from Sturdee's fleet and the WT station at Port Stanley, along with a report from the collier *Amasis* giving the news that, apart from the *Canopus*, there were no British warships at Port Stanley, had convinced the German admiral that the coast was clear and that he could take his time getting to the Falkland Islands.

As it transpired, he was out in his reckoning by a mere twenty four hours. When the German Squadron rounded the Horn, Sturdee was still several days sailing away from the Falklands but von Spee, thinking he had all the time in the world, stopped at Picton Island to take on board more coal. The delay was crucial and by the time his ships finally began to make their approach to Port Stanley, Sturdee had been there for several hours.

Von Spee's intention was to attack the Falkland Islands, destroying the wireless station and causing as much damage as he could. The coal stocks in the port would be more than useful, along with harbour and dock facilities of which his ships were in desperate need. Then, repaired and re-supplied, he would feel considerably better equipped to take his chances on making a clear run up the Atlantic and getting home to Germany. Now, adding to the mistake of delaying his approach to the Falklands, the usually resolute and adroit German commander made another blunder. Falling into the trap of complacency, von

Frederick Charles Doveton Sturdee,
(1859–1925). Sturdee as Vice-Admiral on
board HMS *Hercules* at about the tme
of the Battle of Jutland, 1916. He had
been promoted to Vice-Admiral in 1913.
Following his success at the Falklands
he later commanded the Fourth Battle
Squadron at Jutland, becoming admiral
in 1917.

SMS *Karlsruhe* was a light cruiser of the *Karlsruhe* class built by the *Kaiserliche Marine*. She
had one sister ship, SMS *Rostock*. She was launched in November 1912, and commissioned by
January 1914. Armed with twelve 10.5 cm SK L/45 guns, *Karlsruhe* had a top speed of 28.5 knots
which allowed her to escape from British cruisers during her career. After her commissioning,
Karlsruhe was assigned to overseas duties in the Caribbean. She arrived in the area in July
1914, days before the outbreak of War. Once the war began, she armed the passenger liner SS
Kronprinz Wilhelm, but while the ships were transferring equipment, British ships located them
and pursued *Karlsruhe*. Her superior speed allowed her to escape, after which she operated off
the north-eastern coast of Brazil. While *en route* to attack the shipping lanes to Barbados on 4
November 1914, an internal explosion destroyed her, killing the majority of the crew.

Spee did not send his light cruisers ahead to reconnoitre. It was normal naval practice but by failing to follow the pattern that had served him so well in the past, he made a simple but dreadful mistake, something that would not have been expected from a commander with von Spee's experience. And in the end it was a mistake that was to prove both costly and fatal.

Completely fooled by the radio silence, von Spee made the assumption that Port Stanley was empty and therefore simply dispatched two of his ships to make a preliminary bombardment of the town and port. He and the rest of the Squadron followed on in a leisurely fashion that was strangely reminiscent of Sturdee's journey south. Consequently, just after dawn on 8 December 1914, the *Gneisenau* and *Nürnberg*, operating five or six miles ahead of the squadron, came in sight of Port Stanley.

Communications with Britain were slow and it was almost twelve hours later that Winston Churchill at the Admiralty heard the news. It was five-o-clock at night:–

> I was working in my room at the Admiralty when Admiral Oliver entered with the following telegram. It was from the Governor of the Falkland Islands and ran as follows—'Admiral Spee arrived at daylight this morning with all his ships and is now in action with Admiral Sturdee's whole fleet, which was coaling.' We had had so many unpleasant surprises that these last words sent a shiver up my spine. Had we been taken by surprise and in spite of all our superiority, mauled, unready at anchor?[39]

If the news meant an anxious time for Churchill, then the appearance of the two German ships caused many a flutter of alarm in members of the British fleet. But, more than that, the over-riding emotion was intense excitement as everyone knew the moment of confrontation had finally arrived.

The First Shots

Once Port Stanley hove into view, Captain Julius Maerker of the *Gneisenau* was quickly able to pick out the details of his intended target. The buildings of the town and harbour were still a dull, grey smudge but the wireless masts on the hill above the port were sharply etched against the blue morning sky. Maerker ordered his guns to bear on the town and WT station. He watched in satisfaction as the turrets began to swing around towards land. And then the lookout, far above the bridge and deck, rang through with a message that chilled Maerker to the bone. There were masts, dozens of masts, in the harbour. Maerker held his course. Perhaps they were merchant ships, he thought. Then, when he was at last able to train his binoculars onto Port Stanley, the sight of large tripod masts that told him there were warships in the harbour.

At that moment there were two loud cracks and, moments later, tall spouts of water rose sharply into the air alongside the *Gneisenau* and *Nürnberg*. The old

On the morning of 8 December 1914 two German ships approached Port Stanley, the main town and harbour on the Falklands, little realising that the British were there in force. One was the *Gneisenau*, the other the light cruiser *Nürnberg*.

The *Canopus* at last opens fire! The opening shots of the battle were fired by the old battleship, across a low neck of land, splashing into the water uncomfortably close to the *Gneisenau* and *Nürnberg*. The two German ships immediately turned and fled back to the safety of their Squadron.

Canopus had finally been able to fire the guns on which Churchill had placed so much store. And good shooting it was, too:–

> The two 12 inch guns in the fore turret, elevated to the utmost, were fired together, with one detonating crash—two great columns of spray rose higher than the mastheads of the advancing foe. Three more shots were fired in quick succession at 12,000 yards and, though the survivors of the two ships afterwards admitted that pieces of shell had ricocheted on board, the only effect was to make the enemy turn to starboard and rejoin their Squadron, still specks on the horizon.[40]

Maerker knew that the shots and the sight of tripod masts could mean only one thing. Battle cruisers! But he was equally sure that von Spee would have been informed by the German Admiralty if the British had sent battle cruisers to the area. He also knew that the Japanese had recently adopted tripod masts for their capital ships. Therefore it must be the *Kawachi* and some of the other Japanese warships, currently searching for the East Asiatic Squadron, that were now lying in wait in the harbour.

Maerker immediately signalled von Spee. Over the low strip of land that separated him from the harbour he could see that the battle cruisers were not yet coming out and knew that a determined attack could pay dividends. Von Spee's answer was unequivocal—'Do not accept action.' It was, arguably, yet another terrible mistake on the part of the German admiral. Whichever ships were in Port Stanley harbour, Maerker obeyed von Spee's orders and the *Gneisenau* and *Nürnberg* were soon speeding back towards the security of von Spee and the rest of the German ships.

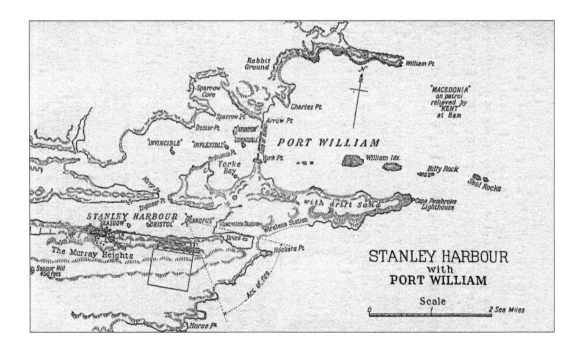

STANLEY HARBOUR
with
PORT WILLIAM

Scale
0   1   2 Sea Miles

Action Stations

To begin with there was utter chaos in the harbour of Port Stanley. With the fleet so recently anchored there was, as yet, no land line between the *Canopus* and the flagship. Not only that, the old battleship was grounded in such a position as to make visual sighting of any signals totally impossible. The situation was not good.

The only ship that had steam up and was ready for action was the *Glasgow*. Both battle cruisers were in the middle of coaling, as were the other armoured cruisers. The *Bristol* had let her fires go out, ready for essential repairs, and the *Cornwall*'s engines had already been partly dismantled.

With the *Glasgow* moored in a position to make visual contact both with the *Canopus* and the *Invincible*, messages—penetrating the shroud of coal dust that shrouded the battle cruiser—were passed using a searchlight. When Sturdee was informed that the enemy was in sight, he was in the middle of shaving but paused to give the order to raise steam. Then he settled down to a hearty breakfast.

Despite his seeming composure, Sturdee's situation was far from secure. Only the *Glasgow* and *Kent*—and she would have required at least an hour before she could sail—were in anything like a position to fight. In the end it took two hours for the battle cruisers clear away the colliers and the remnants of the coal from their decks and be ready for sea.

Playing the 'what if?' game is not usually productive but the question has to be posed—why did von Spee not sit off Port Stanley and shell the virtually helpless British ships at his leisure? It only needed him to sink *Glasgow* or one of the other light cruisers in the entrance to the harbour and the whole of Sturdee's fleet would have been bottled up in port. At the end of the day such questions are immaterial. Von Spee did not attack and now he would have to pay the price.

The British fleet finally weighed anchor just before 10.00 a.m. The *Glasgow*, Captain Luce as eager as ever, was first out, closely followed by the *Kent*. Then came the two battle cruisers, one midshipman in the *Invincible* later recalling:–

> The stokers worked like mad down below. We used our precious oil now that we had got the enemy at last. The funnels belched out dense black smoke and flames, and we up-anchored and rushed out.[41]

In the general confusion and uproar of getting out after the enemy there was little time for niceties. Picket boats were abandoned, sailing pinnaces were cast adrift, stores and provisions left to wallow on the decks of the tiny supply vessels. If anything got in the way of the mad dash to sea, then it was mercilessly mown down:–

> We were tearing out, ramming anything that got in our way. We cut two small boats in half—happily there was no one in them.[42]

The armoured cruiser *Kent*, coaling in the harbour, was one of the first vessels out in pursuit of the German ships. Old and antiquated, she should have been no match for the speedy German ships but her engine room staff worked miracles to get extra speed out of her boilers.

The *Carnarvon* struggled to keep up the pace and quickly fell behind the other British ships as they chased after the German squadron.

An artist's impression of the opening stages to the Battle of the Falkland Islands, the Long Chase as it was known. From left to right—*Glasgow*, *Kent*, *Invincible*, *Inflexible*, *Scharnhorst*, *Gneisenau*, *Nürnberg*, *Dresden* and *Leipzig*.

Once out of harbour, at 10.20 Sturdee signalled 'General Chase' and as the flags climbed to the mastheads there was a loud cheer from the decks of all the British ships. It was time to revenge Kit Craddock and the men who had gone down with him.

8

The Battle of the Falkland Islands

The Long Chase

Captain Maerker and Commander Pochhammer, the First Lieutenant on the *Gneisenau*, now almost back with von Spee and the rest of the squadron, were at last able to see the two battle cruisers clearly. Despite the vast clouds of dark smoke that they were pouring out, the spacing of the three funnels, along with their tripod masts, convinced him that these were British ships. He knew that these vessels were far faster than their Japanese equivalents and, more importantly, that they were considerably faster than his own tired ship. And faster, too, than the rest of the Squadron.

It did not take long for Captain Maerker on *Gneisenau* and Admiral von Spee on the *Scharnhorst* to see that they were being gradually over-hauled. Making a good 26 knots, Sturdee was relentlessly closing the range on the German ships.

It is difficult to know what von Spee was thinking at this crucial moment. He would have realised that he had been out-foxed by the British radio silence and by the speed with which they had assembled this avenging fleet. Did he, perhaps, regret the wasted days when he had dawdled and prevaricated rather than head directly for the Falklands? Whatever he thought, he would have known that death and disaster were now staring him in the face. The two German armoured cruisers, hampered by barnacles and other encrustations, by engines that were desperately in need of overhaul, could make nowhere near the speed of the chasing battle cruisers. While the older armoured cruisers of the British fleet were slowly being left behind, the real danger lay in the shape of the two British capital ships.

Von Spee immediately ordered his Squadron to flee to the south, in a drastic attempt to out-run the British. There was still a faint chance that, if the weather closed in, he could lose Sturdee but the day was fine, the sea calm—at least at this early stage—and, as it turned out, any possibility of shaking off the British was a forlorn hope.

At 12.55 the *Inflexible* opened fire—finding the range as much as anything else—followed closely by the *Invincible* four minutes later. Firing continued

Carnarvon

1.30 P.M.

Scale of Yards.

1000　0　1000　2000　3000　4000　5000　6000　7000　8000　9000　10000　11000

Cornwall

Kent

Inflexible
Glasgow
Invincible

Leipzig
Nürnberg

Gneisenau
Scharnhorst

Dresden

The *Scharnhorst* at speed, trying desperately to get away from the chasing British ships.

Shells exploding in the sea in front of British warships. From the beginning of the battle, right to the end, German gunnery was exemplary.

from both battle cruisers but it was poor shooting, at least for a while. One or two shots fell close to the enemy ships and after several dozen attempts the cruiser *Leipzig* was eventually straddled but, in the main, most of the salvos fell well short.

Sturdee had a following wind and, with oil now being sprayed onto the coal in their boilers to increase speed, the huge quantities of smoke from the battle cruisers threatened to obscure the targets. It was a major problem for the range finders and spotters, throughout the battle. To the men watching on the *Glasgow* and *Kent* it seemed as if their comrades would never manage to hit the German ships.

Having the advantage of speed, Sturdee knew he had to keep his ships out of range of the German 8.2 inch guns while remaining inside the range of his own 12 inch weapons. But that was not easy against a wily opponent like von Spee and for a while what developed was a 'cat and mouse' game of move and counter move from the two forces.

When the distance between the two fleets was down to 16,000 yards, just before 1.30 p.m., von Spee made the decision to split his force. He would turn with *Scharnhorst* and *Gneisenau* to face the battle cruisers and draw their fire onto himself.

It was a courageous move, almost suicidal, but, if successful, it would give the light cruisers—*Nürnberg*, *Leipzig* and *Dresden*—the chance to scatter and run. It was their only hope of survival, von Spee banking on the idea that the British capital ships would concentrate on him. That left the British armoured cruisers, vessels as old as the *Good Hope* and *Monmouth*. His own cruisers, von Spee hoped, would be able to outrun their older opponents.

Sturdee accepted the challenge and immediately signalled that the chase and, he hoped, the eventual destruction of the German light cruisers was down to his own three armoured and one light cruiser. The *Bristol*, in a state of poor repair, had already been dispatched to hunt down the German colliers which had scattered as soon as the British vessels left port. For the two big German ships there was, now, very little hope unless they could outfight and out manoeuvre the battle cruisers. It was 1.20 in the afternoon.

The Main Fight

If the British firing was ineffective, the German gunnery was excellent, right from the start. Both *Scharnhorst* and *Gneisenau* straddled the battle cruisers time after time and at one stage, due to superb handling from von Spee, managed to get the range down to 14,000 yards where their 5.9 inch guns could also be used. It was not long before the *Scharnhorst* scored a hit on the *Invincible*, something that caused Sturdee to turn away and open the range again.

By now there were distinct signs of bad weather on the horizon and when Sturdee was once more forced to turn away—this time in order to clear the

An artist's impression, somewhat romantic and unreal, shows the end of the *Scharnhorst*.

clouds of acrid smoke for his range finders—von Spee seized the chance to put distance between himself and the enemy battle cruisers. He fled south to where he hoped the looming grey clouds and bad weather might shield him. Another chase commenced, this time the lull in firing lasting for forty-five minutes before the Germans were caught and firing began again.

During the height of the battle, a sailing ship suddenly and serenely appeared on the British port beam. It was, apparently, a French barque that had no knowledge of the war but which suddenly found herself in the middle of a dramatic sea fight. For several moments everyone stared at the apparition that had appeared. Then she sailed blithely on and quickly disappeared.

During the break in the firing, one of the midshipmen in the *Invincible*, serving in A Turret and unable to curb his youthful exuberance, decided on an unimpeded view of the affair:–

> I climbed upon the top of the turret to have a look around. Suddenly we altered course and made for the enemy. I now noticed we were closing and when their first salvo went off I was still on the top of the turret. I could see all the shells coming at us, and I felt that they were coming straight at me. However, they all missed, except one which hit the side of the ship near the wardroom, and made a great green flash and sent splinters flying all around. I hopped below armour quickly and started working again.[43]

Both the *Invincible* and *Inflexible* now turned side on to the enemy in order to bring more guns to bear, *Invincible* taking the *Scharnhorst*, *Inflexible* the *Gneisenau*. Von Spee's reply was prompt and turned across the bows of the British ships in a classic 'crossing of the T,' a tactic that had been in use since Nelson's day.

Crossing the T was a highly effective manoeuvre, bringing von Spee's smaller weapons into action. As ever, the German gunnery was magnificent. Most of their hits, however, burst harmlessly on the armour plating of the battle cruisers. In contrast, the British gunnery had now become far more effective and soon the *Scharnhorst*'s firing began to fall away:–

> We hit again and again. First, our left gun sent her big crane spinning over the side. Then our right gun blew her funnel to atoms and then another shot from the left gun sent her bridge and part of the forecastle sky high. We were not escaping free, however. Shots were hitting us repeatedly—Suddenly a great livid flame rushed through the gun ports, and splinters flew all round, and we felt the 150 or 200 tons of the turret going up in the air. We thought we would go over the side and get drowned like rats in a trap. However, we came down again with a crash that shook the turret dreadfully, and continued firing as hard as ever.[44]

Fires had broken out at various points on the *Scharnhorst*, the ship having taken at least forty direct hits from heavy shells, and most of her guns were now out of action. Bodies of the dead and dying lay strewn about the deck but von Spee was still alive. His last message was a generous one—'You were right,' he signalled to Maerker in the *Gneisenau*. Maerker had been opposed all along to the attack on the Falklands—or von Spee might have been referring to his decision not to attack the British ships before they had cleared Port Stanley. Either way, it was too late now.

When the end came, it came quickly. The German flagship was ablaze from stem to stern but she was still firing steadily with those guns that remained in action:–

> I could see she was in a bad way. She was down by the bows and badly on fire amidships—I saw the *Scharnhorst*'s ensign dip (never knew whether it came down or not, because just then one of our lyddite shells hit her and there was a dense cloud of smoke all over her). When it cleared she was on her side, and her propellers were lashing the water into foam. Then she capsized altogether and went to the bottom.[45]

Like the *Good Hope* and *Monmouth* before her, the *Scharnhorst* went down with all hands, 900 men including Admiral Maximilian von Spee.

The *Gneisenau* continued to fight on although she, too, was now blazing furiously. Both British battle cruisers as well as the *Carnarvon* which was too slow to chase the fleeing German cruisers, concentrated their fire on the battered ship and the damage was awful to see.

Soon only one gun was working but the Germans continued to battle on, even though Sturdee had ordered his own ships to cease fire. Her ensign flying to the end, the *Gneisenau* finally turned onto her side and slid below the ice cold waves. The Germans opened the sea cocks on their ship in order to help her in her death throes:–

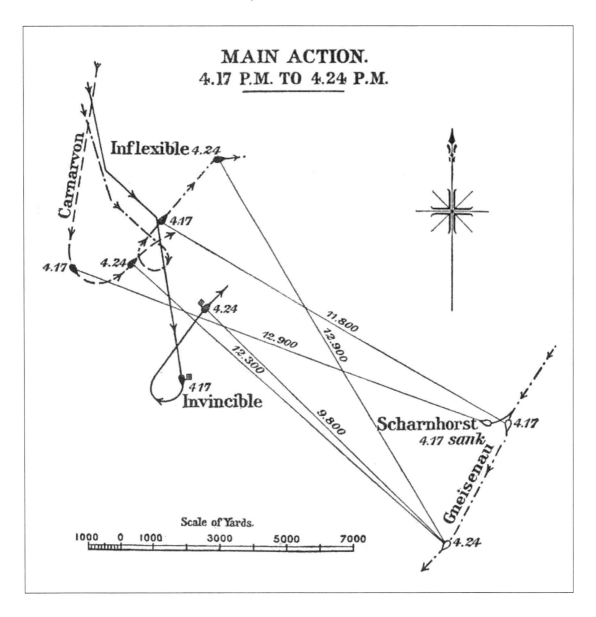

MAIN ACTION.
4.17 P.M. TO 4.24 P.M.

Not able to keep up with the other cruisers, the *Carnarvon* added her guns to the weight of fire pouring down onto the two German armoured cruisers from the *Invincible* and *Inflexible*. This view shows *Carnarvon* at Malta before the war.

Picking up survivors was difficult as both British battlecruisers had had their boats holed in the battle but some attempts were made. This shows survivors from the *Gneisenau* in the water, one of the battlecruisers in the background.

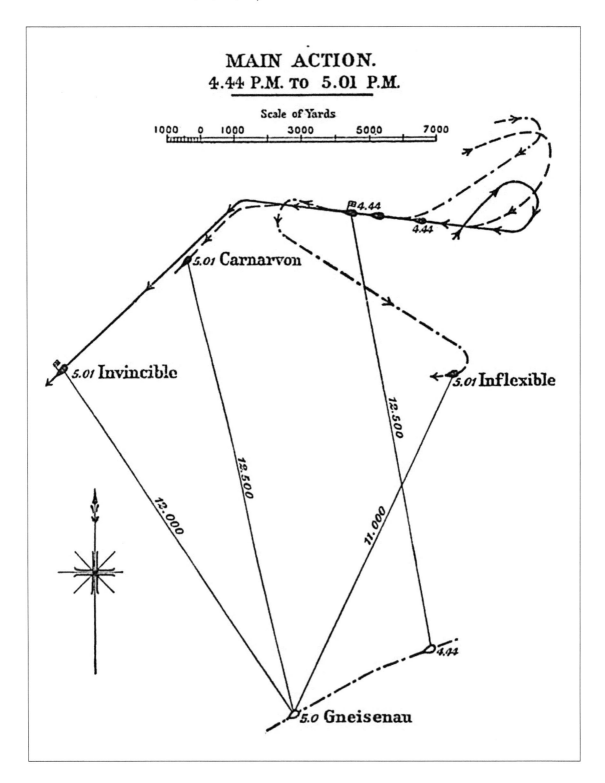

MAIN ACTION.
4.44 P.M. TO 5.01 P.M.

More *Gneisenau* survivors are helped as the British sailors line the decks to watch and help. In the end about 200 men were pulled from the water.

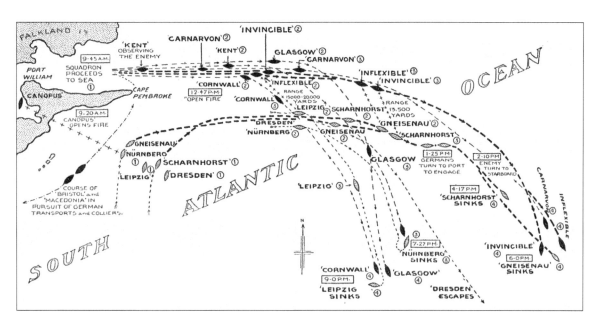

The numbers on the plan give the corresponding positions of the vessels at various times. All ships bearing the same number were simultaneously in the positions charted. The heavy dotted lines indicate the course of the battle cruisers and German armoured cruisers. The thin dotted lines indicate the course taken by the light cruisers.

When we came near we could see that the water was all yellow where she had sunk and there was a dreadful smell of lyddite in the air. It was absolutely dreadful and what with all those wretched Germans drowning and sending up pitiful cries for help, which we could not give because most of our boats were in splinters, I hope I shall never have to go through it again.[46]

The *Invincible* and *Inflexible* did eventually manage to launch a few undamaged boats and were able to pick up some 200 survivors. Many of them had open wounds, limbs missing or mauled, and the ravaging skuas and other giant sea birds that came diving in on the injured men had to be beaten off by the rescuers.

Captain Maerker, like his friend and colleague Admiral von Spee, went down with his ship. Commander Hans Pochhamer was one of those pulled from the water, the most senior German officer to survive the sinking of the two armoured cruisers. He was given a cabin on board the *Inflexible*, treated as an honoured guest and later wrote a book on his experiences.

As the rescue operation continued, thick cloud and a dense mist finally began to steal in over the scene of the battle, a few hours too late to help von Spee but a fitting blanket to hide the carnage that had just taken place.

Destroying the Cruisers

The *Gneisenau* sank a little after 6.00 p.m. At that stage the German light cruisers were still afloat and were all still ahead of the pursing British ships, all still trying desperately to find the sanctuary and the safety for which their admiral had sacrificed his life.

Early on in the chase, Captain Luce of the *Glasgow*—the senior British officer on board the chasing cruisers—had decided that the *Kent* should concentrate on the *Nürnberg*, leaving *Cornwall*—and perhaps himself—to fight the *Leipzig*.

Engines racing, firemen stripped to the waist, the *Kent* was soon in hot pursuit of the *Nürnberg* but was being gradually outpaced and left behind. It was beginning to look for all the world as if the German ship would soon disappear into the gloom of a South Atlantic evening. Then, fate played a hand. Pressing for extra speed, the German vessel blew two of her boilers. Her speed dropped and everyone knew the end was not far away. The *Nürnberg*'s guns had easily out-ranged the British ship in the early part of the duel but now the *Kent* closed in to fight at close quarters. As ever, German gunnery was exemplary.

One of *Nürnberg*'s shells burst in a casement on the *Kent*, killing six men and wounding several others. Cordite was ignited and only prompt action by Marine Sergeant Charles Mayes, who picked up the burning charge and ran with it in his arms to deposit it in a bucket of water—before flooding the compartment—saved the ship. He was later awarded the DCM for his bravery.

For more than an hour and a half the battle continued to rage. The *Kent* closed to within 3,000 yards and as the salvos flew and shrapnel peppered the

HMS *Kent* passes the sunken remains of the *Nürnberg* as, in the most bizarre of incidents, a four-masted barque appears out of the mist before disappearing into the distance. From a painting by W. L. Wyllie

The armoured cruiser *Cornwall*, allocated the *Leipzig* to chase and destroy by John Luce, the senior British cruiser Captain.

superstructure, her foremast was cut through and swung loose. But at this close range the heavier guns of the British ship at last began to take their toll. Soon the *Nürnberg*'s funnel was riddled with holes and, one by one, her guns fell silent.

The amount of punishment taken by the cruiser, with shells raining down onto her decks, amazed the British sailors. As Captain J. D. Allen of the *Kent* later wrote in his diary—'It is hard to understand how the *Nürnberg* could survive it so long.' Survive it she did and minute succeeded minute in the agonizing death throes of the ship and her crew.

Just when it seemed that the *Nürnberg* could take no more, the four masted barque that had appeared earlier in the battle suddenly re-appeared. She came ghosting out of the mist and then, as sailors from both sides stared in amazement at this vessel from a different time, from a different world, she sailed serenely on and disappeared into the gloom.

Quite what the seamen on board the sailing ship thought of the battle that was unfolding in front of them is not known. Sailors are superstitious beings, however, and the men on the *Kent* were quite clear—this was no ordinary four master, this was the ghost ship that often appeared during British naval battles.

With the *Nürnberg* now on fire and almost dead in the water, the *Kent* stopped shooting but the German ensign still flew and, reluctantly, Captain Allen ordered that firing should recommence. Finally the signal 'Do you surrender?' was made and with the *Nürnberg* clearly sinking, the ensign came down at last. There was a palpable sense of relief on the British ship, everyone knowing that *Nürnberg* would have to take no more punishment:–

> It is near dusk now, 7.30, and we have been two hours in action. Up comes everyone from below, from casements and turrets to stare and rejoice; but they are all immediately hustled away to do what can be done to save life. All our boats are riddled, and none of them can be repaired for an hour. So we do what we can with lifebuoys and lumps of wood paid astern but it's mighty little; it's a loppy sea and dreadfully cold.[47]

As the *Nürnberg* finally sank below the waves one German sailor stood erect on the shattered hull and defiantly waved the ship's battle ensign in the air. He went down with the ship.

Sinking the Leipzig

With the German cruisers racing away in a lop-sided V formation—*Dresden* in the centre, *Nürnberg* to port and *Leipzig* to starboard—it had soon became clear that none of the British cruisers, with the possible exception of *Glasgow*, would be nearly fast enough to get within range, let alone come abreast of the *Dresden*. The *Leipzig*, however, was a different matter and when the German ships began to spread out in an attempt to disrupt the pursuit, Captain Luce was quick to see that this was his chance.

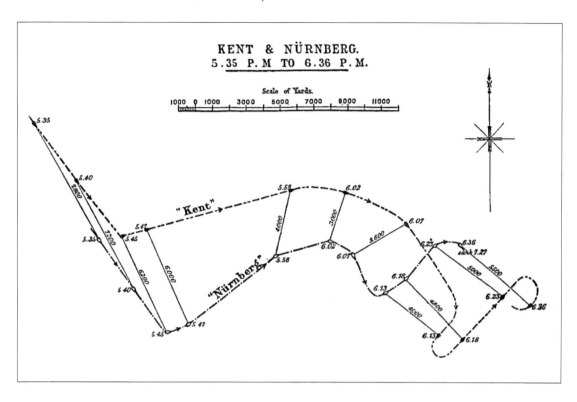

A German postcard depicting the last moments of the *Nürnberg* and the defiant German sailor who stood on the sinking hull and waved the ensign to the last.

The *Leipzig*, shown here just before the war, coaling in San Francisco harbour. Coaling was a back-breaking task that was hated by all sailors but was essential to all steam driven ships.

The *Cornwall* at anchor, battle over.

A newspaper cutting showing battle damage to the cruiser *Kent* which suffered more hits from enemy shells than any other British ship in the battle.

Captain Haun of the *Leipzig* was clearly trying to make for the Argentine coast but *Glasgow* spotted the move and headed him off. Luce knew that his was the only ship fast enough to catch the *Dresden* but in order to get to her he would have to pass the *Leipzig* on the way. With *Kent* and *Cornwall* still some way behind, he decided to fight the *Leipzig* from long range, to hold and delay her until the heavier guns of the *Cornwall* could be brought to bear.

When the range fell to 12,000 yards, *Glasgow* opened fire. By 3.15 p.m. the range was down to 9,000, both *Glasgow* and *Leipzig* now firing with some accuracy. Shooting with her forward six inch gun, the *Glasgow* repeatedly caused the German ship to turn and reply with her full broadside. The manoeuvre delayed the *Leipzig* just long enough to make the eventual outcome something of a foregone conclusion. By now Captain Haun had given up all hope of running for the Argentine coast. With *Glasgow* already firing and *Cornwall* coming up fast, the only option was to fight to the last.

The old *Cornwall* was making a magnificent effort to catch up, her engines powering her through the waves at a speed her designers could only have dreamed about. Captain Walter Ellerton demanded even more speed—and the stokers gave him what he wanted. And before long the *Cornwall* was in action:–

> We are nearly within range of *Leipzig* and soon biff off the fore turret at her, and some little tongues of flame, followed thirty seconds later by splashes several hundred yards away, show that she is returning the compliment.[48]

Fire on the German ship broke out early on in the action. Sterling work by the damage control parties prevented it spreading further but no-one could

Shell damage to the *Kent*. The sailors of the *Nürnberg*, which she fought, showed courage and dedication to the last—and were extremely accurate with their gun fire.

get near the seat of the fire and Haun was soon forced to drop his speed. It meant that the British cruisers could now circle and then pummel *Leipzig* at their leisure. John Luce, who would have dearly loved to pursue and sink the *Dresden*—already hull down on the horizon— knew that he had no option but to stay until the *Leipzig* was finally dispatched.

Both *Glasgow* and *Cornwall* were hit many times but as the rain for which von Spee had been praying finally swept in, the *Cornwall* scored a decisive hit that carried away the *Leipzig*'s foretop, wrecked her fire control and killed the Gunnery Officer. Gradually, in what was really a battle of attrition, the *Leipzig* was reduced to a complete wreck.

At Luce's orders, lyddite was now used by the British ships. *Leipzig*'s speed slackened even more and her gun fire virtually died away. Her ammunition almost exhausted—2,000 rounds having been fired during the engagement—and with all rangefinders destroyed, the ship's officers were forced aim the few remaining shells by eyesight.

In a last desperate attempt to take one of the enemy with him, Captain Haun launched torpedoes but the *Glasgow* was too far away and the missiles sped harmlessly past.

Time and time again, Captain Luce had pleaded with the *Leipzig* to surrender but there was no response. Finally, just after 7.30 p.m. there was a massive explosion on the German cruiser and, with the ship's sea cocks opened, the crew came on deck. There was still no indication of surrender and, afraid of another torpedo attack, Luce was obliged to fire another salvo.

With the sea now shrouded in the funereal blackness of a South Atlantic night, the *Leipzig* fired a green flare and the two British cruisers closed in to try to rescue all the men they could find. It was not many as their boats had been damaged and only six German sailors were eventually pulled from the sea. Captain Haun, who had been walking about the deck, encouraging his men and giving out cigarettes, was not one of them. He was last seen walking calmly towards the shattered bridge, smoking a final cigar.

The Escape of the Dresden

By the time *Leipzig* and *Nürnberg* had been sunk, there was no sign of the fleeing *Dresden*. Captain Lüdecke always seemed to have more than his fair share of luck. He had, after all, exchanged commands with Köhler just before the war began, leaving the younger man to sail the *Karlsruhe* to her mysterious destruction in the West Indies. And now he had vanished into the endless wilds of the Atlantic.

The *Carnarvon* had gamely tried to follow her but the old armoured cruiser had no chance of staying with the *Dresden*, one of the fastest vessels in the German Squadron.

As the *Carnarvon* finally gave up the futile chase, her crew could do little more than record that *Dresden* had disappeared to the south-west. But what course she took when she was below the horizon was anybody's guess.

Glasgow and *Cornwall* immediately attempted to search but lack of coal—they had been in the process of re-coaling when the German squadron first appeared—soon forced them to return from the Magellan Straits to the Falkland Islands. Admiral Sturdee took up the reins and headed south-west with his two battle cruisers.

Sturdee was no more fortunate than Luce and Ellerton. A thick mist soon descended over the area, totally preventing a systematic and detailed search pattern. Consequently, on 10 December, the day after the battle, he gave it up for a bad job and returned to Port Stanley.

The *Bristol* had quickly dispatched two of the German colliers but one had somehow managed to elude her. If the battle had not resulted in total annihilation of von Spee's force then it missed only by a hairsbreadth. Out of von Spee's dangerous squadron just one light cruiser and one collier remained at liberty. The defeat may not have meant much in terms of ships lost and men killed but it was a huge blow to German morale after the success of Coronel. From a position where it had seemed as if Germany might actually rule the oceans of the southern hemisphere, the Royal Navy was now totally dominant once more.

Aftermath

Despite his mistakes before the final battle, the death of Admiral von Spee deprived Germany of a supreme tactician and it is interesting to ponder what he might have achieved had he been able to make it back to Germany. Defeat at the Falkland Islands also cost the life of both von Spee's sons. Otto von Spee went down with the *Nürnberg* while Heinrich von Spee was drowned when the *Gneisenau* was finally sunk. The deaths left the von Spee family with just daughters to carry on the line.

A total of just over 2,000 German sailors were lost in the action, several hundred more being pulled from the water and taken prisoner. They were ordinary sailors, men with wives and families, but they had fought with matchless courage that even their enemies were quick to acknowledge and praise.

British losses were light, no more than a handful—ten dead, fifteen wounded. To the strategists and naval planners at the Admiralty, it did not seem a huge toll and compared to the significance of the victory, it was probably a price worth paying.

For Britain, the defeat of von Spee had significant strategic consequences. Troop convoys could now be made once again from Australia, South Africa and New Zealand without any fear of interruption, something that was vital for the waging of the land war on the Western Front. British morale was lifted by the success, a very important matter after the bitter hurt of Coronel. Kit Craddock had been avenged in the most devastating fashion, causing Admiral Beatty to later call the victory the most decisive naval battle of the war.

Die beiden Söhne des Admirals Graf von Spee
Leutnant Graf Otto von Spee   Leutnant Graf Heinrich von Spee
an Bord S. M. S. „Nürnberg"   und   an Bord S. M. S. „Gneisenau"
starben den Heldentod in der Seeschlacht bei den Falklands-Inseln
am 8. Dezember 1914.

5186

F. Urbahns,
Hofphot.
Kiel

The sons of Admiral Spee, Otto who served on SMS *Nürnberg*, and Heinrich who served on SMS *Gneisenau*.

Three members of the von Spee family died at the Falkland Islands—Admiral Maximilian von Spee and his sons Otto and Heinrich on the *Nürnberg* and *Gneisenau* respectively. This German postcard commemorates their sacrifice.

Winston Churchill was also delighted with the outcome. Always a broad brush stroke player, it did not matter to him that the *Dresden* had escaped. She could be dealt with later. Churchill understood the global position only too well:–

> It had taken four months from the beginning of the war to achieve this result. Its consequences were far reaching, and affected simultaneously our position in every part of the globe. The strain was everywhere relaxed.[49]

The performance of the battle cruisers had been clinical and totally effective. As the admiral and man in charge of the avenging fleet Sturdee naturally took much of the credit. He was also praised for the work of his three major cruiser Captains—Luce of the *Glasgow*, Allen of the *Kent* and Ellerton of the *Cornwall*—but they could only ever be as good as the man who directed and commanded their operations, in this case Admiral Frederick Doveton Sturdee.

For Allen and Ellerton, in particular, to pursue, catch and destroy the *Nürnberg* and *Leipzig* in two armoured cruisers that were virtually obsolete long before war broke out was nothing short of a minor miracle. Admiral Sturdee knew that and was fulsome in his praise of subordinates.

It was not all sweetness and light, however. Jacky Fisher, never one of Sturdee's greatest admirers, could not find it in him to praise the admiral. Instead he bitterly resented the fact that *Dresden* had escaped and chose to heap blame for this 'failure' on Sturdee.

To rub salt in the wounds, Sturdee had achieved his victory using two of Fisher's babies, the battle cruisers *Invincible* and *Inflexible*. Jacky Fisher had originated the battle cruiser concept several years before and to see his despised subordinate—hated might be going a little far—bring it to glorious conclusion was almost more than he could bear.

The *Dresden* was a good stick with which to beat Sturdee. At one stage Fisher even suggested that he should not be allowed to return home until he had hunted down and destroyed the *Dresden*. Not only that, Fisher's suggestion was that the battle cruisers should be returned to the Grand Fleet and Sturdee left to carry out the hunt in the aged and totally unsuitable *Carnarvon*. It was never really an option but it does illustrate the black and bitter venom of which Jacky Fisher was capable.

Eventually, Fisher made so many repeated demands, asking why the last German cruiser had been allowed to get away, why Sturdee had expended so many shells in the action, why the German collier had been allowed to escape and so on, that the victorious admiral was stung into a response. He made a formal reply to the Admiralty, calling Fisher's attitude unexpected and unhelpful. Fisher fell back on his dignity and on the safety of his position as Sturdee's superior officer. His rebuke was both sullen and undignified.

When the admiral finally returned to Britain at the beginning of 1915, he was awarded a rather luke-warm five minute interview with Churchill—undoubtedly under pressure from his friend—and with Fisher. The First Sea Lord was never one to hide his enmity and this time he even went as far as to ignore many of Sturdee's recommendations for honours, a sad and uncalled for snub for brave men who were caught up in Fisher's personal vendetta.

It did not matter. To the British public Sturdee was the hero of the hour—even more reason for him to incur Fisher's wrath—and Parliament duly awarded him a baronetcy, along with a cash reward of ten thousand pounds. It was the first time that a baronetcy as a reward for success in a naval action had been given since the Napoleonic Wars and was undoubtedly well deserved. Jacky Fisher must have been biting his lip in frustration.

9

Mopping up

The Fall of Tsingtao

On 23 August 1914, Japan had given Germany an ultimatum, demanding that the port of Tsingtao—although, technically, in Chinese territory—be ceded to Japanese forces. It was ignored and the German garrison prepared for a long and gruelling siege, although no-one on either side was ever really in doubt about the ultimate outcome. Far from home, isolated and alone, with no hope of relief, the German forces could only fight until the end and soon after the deadline for the ultimatum ran out the Japanese siege began.

In the middle of September 1914 the old battleship *Triumph* had been detached from Admiral Jerram's command at Hong Kong and ordered to join the Japanese blockading fleet. She went to sea in a typhoon but a few days later she and the destroyer *Usk* joined the Japanese force gathered off the German-held port. She spent the next few weeks escorting convoys and bombarding the German emplacements.

The German gunners replied in kind:–

> A spotting officer, who was in a barrel lashed to the foremast, an advantageous if dangerous position, writes as his comment: 'Our shells burst all over the place, and appeared to set fire to a village and quantities of brushwood—The shells make a loud whistling noise as they came, and fall with a plop into the water. One's instinct makes one duck one's head, which is rather comic when one comes to think of it.'[50]

On 29 September a representative of the Japanese Emperor arrived with the fleet. He came on board the *Triumph*, made the usual speech and presented the ship with five dozen bottles of saki. It was a brief respite from the seemingly interminable process of steaming out to sea for the night, followed by a return in shore and further bombardments during the day.

Balloons and spotting aircraft were used by both sides during the siege and during one intense bombardment the *Triumph* received a 'near miss' from the shore batteries. In late October, a report that the *Scharnhorst* and von Spee's

Squadron were in the vicinity caused the *Triumph* and several Japanese vessels to abandon the siege and head out to sea in the hope of finding the enemy but it was a fruitless search and the blockade was soon re-established.

By 30 October the Japanese land forces were close to the heart of the German defences and the naval forces intensified their bombardment. Still the German garrison held out. The weather on this exposed section of the coast also played a part in the siege:–

> Bad weather raged for four days, and neither the troops nor the ships were able to resume operations. As a suggestive interlude, on Guy Fawkes' Day an effigy of the Kaiser was burnt with great ceremony in the wardroom of the *Triumph*, during the temporary cessation of hostilities.[51]

The following day, 6 November 1914, the besieged garrison, town and port finally surrendered. For the Japanese it was a moment of great triumph but to the Germans it was a stunning blow to their prestige and to their pretensions of power in the Far East.

The necessary message of explanation from Meyer Waldeck, the Governor of Tsingtao, to the Kaiser was short but explicit:–

> To Your Majesty The Kaiser—Fortress has capitulated after exhaustion of means of defence through assault and by means of defences having been breached—Forts and towns beforehand thoroughly harassed by continuous bombardment from the heaviest weapons assisted by heavy bombardment from sea.[52]

Hunting the Dresden

The significance of the *Dresden* was more emotional than physical. She was a light cruiser, armed with just ten 4.1 inch guns and a few torpedo tubes, a ship already battered by months of hard sailing. She might prove troublesome as a raider, as *Emden* had done, but, more importantly for the British and the Admiralty, she was the sole survivor of von Spee's Squadron and therefore needed to be dispatched with all speed. It was, of course, far easier said than done.

Despite Jacky Fisher's threat to keep him in the southern hemisphere, Admiral Sturdee soon sailed for home with his two battle cruisers, leaving the hunt for the elusive sister ship of the *Emden* in the hands of Admiral Stoddart. The search was to be long and protracted.

Dresden's commander, Captain Fritz Emil von Lüdecke, took her around the Horn on the day after the Falklands Battle and on a snow-blown winter's day the ship made the difficult and dangerous passage through the narrow channel into Shell Bay. She was now desperately short of fuel, holding under 200 tons of coal in her bunkers, and with communications being so poor, Lüdecke had no idea what his masters in Berlin wanted him to do.

He knew that he could not risk the Atlantic. That way lay certain destruction. Lacking definite orders, he decided that his best option was to flout the neutrality of Chile—far less friendly now that von Spee had gone—and lurk amongst the creeks and fiords of South America for as long as he was able. The threat of *Dresden*'s presence might well cause undue alarm and panic in the ranks of merchant shipping.

Crewmen were sent ashore to cut wood on the dark and forbidding headlands around Shell Bay. It was not coal but, for the time being, it would have to do. For several days the sailors worked at their task, felling trees and cutting the logs into small pieces able to fit into the ship's boilers. On 12 December Lüdecke finally left Shell Bay for Puntas Arenas where he was at last able to coal from a German collier. One of Lüdecke's officers, Lieutenant William Canaris, used his powers of persuasion on Chilean authorities to grant the *Dresden* a thirty-six hour stay in order for her to stock up with as much coal as possible.

Canaris was a capable and efficient officer who later achieved fame as the head of the Abwehr, the German intelligence service during the Second World War. The 'little admiral,' as he was then called, ran a largely ineffective and inefficient spy network and campaign against Britain, possibly because he secretly opposed the Nazi regime, despising Adolf Hitler and all he stood for. In 1943 he was sacked from his post and, having been implicated in the bomb plot against Hitler, was executed a few days before the war ended.

The fort at Tsingtau after the naval and land bombardments had finished. Surrender of the garrison was inevitable.

In 1914, however, he was largely responsible for making sure the *Dresden* was at least partially equipped to continue the fight. In the New Year of 1915 the *Dresden* transferred to the remote and desolate anchorage of Christmas Bay. Surrounded now by snow-clad mountains, Lüdecke and his ship were, for the moment, quite safe as, on British charts, the bay was shown as solid land.

The British cruisers, *Kent*, *Glasgow*, *Bristol* and *Cornwall*, were still in the area. They had re-fuelled after the battle and were now combing the seas for the *Dresden*. They were soon joined by *Carnarvon*. In what was an infuriating near miss that left everyone cursing their luck, in mid-December the *Bristol* called at Puntas Arenas just fifteen hours after the *Dresden* had left for Christmas Bay. After that, hidden in her secluded anchorage and shielded by the fall and sweep of the southernmost Andes as they tumbled into the sea, there was to be no word of the fugitive German cruiser for several weeks.

By February the strain on the crew was beginning to show. It was not so much the work of maintaining the ship and keeping watch for the British hunters, gruelling and back-breaking though it was, but rather the feelings of despair and uncertainty that weighed like a shroud on their minds. Lüdecke knew, it was time to move. He would head out across the Indian Ocean, he decided, and begin life as a commerce raider.

On 14 February, as a fierce snowstorm swept across the bay, the *Dresden* pulled up her anchor and headed for the open sea.

The End of the Affair

Despite foul weather, throughout the early part of the year the British cruisers continued the search, *Kent*, *Bristol* and *Glasgow* taking up the northern station on the Chilean coast. Then the *Bristol* hit a submerged rock and was forced to return to the Falkland Islands for repair. Reports of *Dresden* sightings came in regularly but there was nothing substantial before the *Bristol* was repaired and able to rejoin the squadron.

Meanwhile the *Dresden* had stopped and sunk the sailing barque *Conway Castle*, her first and only victim, and had managed to take on coal from the *Sierra Cordoba*. The collier was then dispatched for Valparaiso to load more coal while *Dresden* continued to hug the Chilean coast.

The hunting British cruisers had split up, in order to widen their search, when on 3 March Captain Allen of the *Kent* received a message to join the rest of the force in the Pacific. He was, at the time, searching in Cockburn Channel, a narrow and dangerous passageway that was, sometimes, no more than 100 yards wide. Allen's charts were basic and he was unsure of the depth of water. But he got through and once out in the open sea, he felt able to relax.

And then, during the afternoon watch of 8 March, a three funnelled cruiser was spotted on the horizon. It was the *Dresden*. The German ship fled, followed by *Kent*, and despite being high in the water—a clear indication that her coal

The last survivor of von Spee's Squadron, this shows the *Dresden* on fire at Juan Fernandez Island after she had been hunted down and attacked in March 1915.

supplies were low—she began to pull away. Soon she was hull down and the *Kent*, also extremely low on coal but her funnels glowing red in the afternoon sky, lost her in the darkness.

Out of sight at last, Captain Lüdecke headed for Juan Fernandez Island, the lonely spot where Alexander Selkirk, the presumed model for Defoe's Robinson Crusoe had supposedly once spent time. He barely made it. When she dropped anchor *Dresden* had less than a hundred tons of coal on board and her engines, overworked in the chase and by months of endless cruising, were virtually finished. To Lüdecke and his other senior officers, it was the end of the game.

Lüdecke had received permission from the Kaiser to seek internment but he knew, through picking up WT signals, that the enemy was fast approaching. The *Kent*, *Glasgow* and the armed merchant cruiser *Orama* rendezvoused just after dawn some twelve miles south of Juan Fernandez on Sunday 14 March and not long afterwards they came in sight of their quarry.

They were in Chilean waters and *Dresden* was supposedly free from attack but Luce, the senior British officer, decided on aggressive action. Steaming into the anchorage, *Kent* and *Glasgow* opened fire, taking care not to allow any stray shots to over-shoot the target and hit houses in the town. For a few minutes the *Dresden* returned their fire but soon most of her crew fled for the shore. A white flag fluttered to the masthead of the German cruiser and an officer was rowed over to the *Glasgow* to negotiate terms.

Luce refused any form of surrender other than unconditional and threatened to open fire again if this was not promptly agreed. He need not have worried. Lüdecke had no intention of surrendering. The white flag was purely a delaying tactic, explosive charges being laid against the *Dresden*'s hull and the sea cocks opened.

Within minutes the charges exploded and the *Dresden*, her battle ensign now flying again, sank slowly by the bows. The German crew, standing along the shore line, cheered as she gradually disappeared. They were then incarcerated by the Chilean authorities.

First Aid from the British ships was given to the wounded and the most serious cases were embarked on the *Orama* and taken to Valparaiso. Only eight men had been killed in the brief fight but several more had been injured. A Chilean fisherman and boat owner claimed compensation for his cargo of lobsters—the claim settled on the spot with gold sovereigns—but other than that there was no damage done:–

> The *Kent* lived on lobsters for days to come while *Glasgow*'s crew amused them-selves with the only captured survivor from the *Dresden*, the ship's pig who being both hairy and truculent was appropriately called 'Tirpitz.'[53]

The pig became a great favourite with the sailors and was eventually brought back to Britain where it was sold to make money for the Red Cross.

Captain Lüdecke seems to have suffered some sort of breakdown during the loss of his ship and effective management of the interned crew was taken over by Lieutenant Canaris. The young man carried out his task to the best of his ability and then later escaped from his internment camp and made his way back to Germany.

The Chilean government demanded some form of explanation for the violation of her neutrality and were rewarded with a letter of apology from Sir Edward Grey, the British Foreign Minister. It was a small price to pay for the destruction of the final vessel in Admiral von Spee's Squadron. The wreck of the *Dresden* still lies in the harbour on Juan Fernandez.

Players Departing the Stage

Throughout the various campaigns in the southern hemisphere, the German sailors had, almost without exception, conducted themselves with courage and fortitude. Many of them, like Admiral von Spee and Julius Maerker, had died carrying out their duty. The others, in particular the ones who defied all the odds and made it home—men like von Mücke, Lauterbach and Canaris—showed initiative and daring that were in the best traditions of the German Navy.

And then, of course, there were the hundreds of ordinary German seamen, men whose names would never make the history books. Ultimately, they had no choice but to obey orders. And yet they, like their officers, did not question what they were asked to do, or why. They accepted the direction of their superiors, got on with the job in hand and, in many cases, died while doing it. Without doubt, they were the real heroes of the long and cruel campaign.

Damage to the *Dresden* can be seen in this photograph. Attacked by the *Glasgow* and *Kent*, even though she was technically in neutral waters, the German crew scuttled their ship and went happily into captivity.

An artist's view of the final battle against the *Dresden*. It shows rather more open water than was really there but is otherwise accurate in that it does depict *Glasgow* in the lead followed by *Kent* and the AMC *Orama*.

SMS *Dresden* showing the white flag from the foremast shortly before the captain blew up the fore magazine.

Armoured cruiser HMS *Kent*, seen in Esquimalt Harbour, a sheltered body of water in Greater Victoria, British Columbia, Canada. Following her action against SMS *Dresden*, HMS *Kent* headed north for repairs in these quiet waters. She was briefly assigned to the China Station later in March before returning to the United Kingdom in May.

Courage was not just a German preserve. Kit Craddock and his crews went into battle knowing that their ships were out-dated and out-classed, knowing they had little or no chance of survival. Yet they did not falter and, even when death stared them in the face, they continued to fight, to do their duty to the end.

Sturdee, despite his altercation with Jacky Fisher and those in authority at the Admiralty, prospered. He commanded the 4th Battle Cruiser Squadron at the Battle of Jutland and at the end of the war became Commander in Chief at the Nore. In 1921 he was made Admiral of the Fleet but retired through ill health and died on 7 May 1924.

John Luce, a man in the best traditions of frigate captains from the sailing ship days of the Napoleonic Wars, became Commander of the RNAS base at Cranwell and in 1919 took command of the battleship *Ramillies*. Like Ellerton and Allen, his colleagues on the *Cornwall* and *Kent*, he achieved flag rank in the years after the war. By 1921 he was admiral in charge of Malta and, following his retirement, became High Sheriff of Wiltshire. He died in September 1932.

Jacky Fisher perished—professionally, at least—as he had lived, by the sword. His own sword. He quarrelled with his friend and mentor Winston Churchill over the conduct of the Gallipoli Campaign and then, in May 1915, he went a step too far. Always certain of his own worth, he wrote a stern, even vitriolic, letter to Herbert Asquith, the Prime Minister. In it he outlined his demands, things he would need in place if he was to stay on as First Sea Lord. Otherwise he would resign. Confidently expecting Asquith to agree to everything, Fisher left London for his home in Scotland. On the platform of Crewe Station he was met by the Station Master with a telegram in his hand. Asquith had accepted his resignation. Fisher subsided into an unhappy retirement and died in 1920.

The bungled Gallipoli Campaign also saw the demise of Churchill, its arch-planner. He was certain that, if it had been better handled, Gallipoli and the Dardanelles would have been a success but with over 250,000 casualties he was left with no alternative other than to resign his post at the Admiralty. He would, of course, return but his final comment on the matter was made with typical Churchillian pomp and verbal eloquence— 'I came—I saw—I capitulated.'[54]

And the ships? All of the German vessels, from the cruisers of von Spee's Squadron to individual raiders, from supply ships to armed merchant cruisers were, by the summer of 1915, either resting on the sea bed or interned in neutral ports. They had performed magnificently, way beyond anything that was ever expected of them but, as von Spee had known all along, in the end they were over-whelmed by superior forces. None of them survived the winter of 1914-18—apart from the *Königsberg* and more will be heard of her in the next and final chapter.

British ships on the other hand went on to further action and glory. The *Canopus* was soon rescued from her lonely isolation on the mud of Port Stanley harbour. She was given no time to rest on her laurels as the first ship to fire a shot at the Battle of the Falkland Islands but on 18 December was whisked away, firstly to the Albrohos Rocks where she was to act as guard ship and then to the

Dardanelles where she played a vital role in the Gallipoli campaign, bombarding the Turkish positions. She finished her active service life as a depot ship.

The *Invincible* and *Inflexible*, the twin destroyers of von Spee's armoured cruisers, quickly returned to the Grand Fleet but from there their fortunes took rather different paths. The *Invincible* was sunk at the Battle of Jutland, one of several battle cruisers that blew up thanks to the policy of leaving open doors in the ammunition hoists during action, causing Admiral Beatty to utter his famous remark 'There's something wrong with our bloody ships today.' Indeed there was and a lot of it was down to Beatty's mishandling of those ships.

Inflexible also served at Jutland but escaped unscathed. She was not so lucky at Gallipoli where she was mined and seriously damaged. Despite this mishap, she survived the war only to be scrapped in 1920.

The *Kent* was scrapped the same year, after service at Vladivostock, helping the White Russian forces to fight the Bolsheviks, while the *Cornwall* spent the rest of the war on convoy duties in the Atlantic. The *Glasgow*, survivor of both Coronel and the Falklands battles, was sent to the Mediterranean and was sold out of the Navy in 1926.

The armoured cruiser *Defence*, which had played a peripheral but important role in the tragedy of Kit Craddock and his Squadron at Coronel, fought at Jutland and exploded in a ball of flame when she was hit by a salvo from one of Admiral Hipper's battle cruisers. There were no survivors.

Men and ships, crucial elements in the campaigns in the southern hemisphere. The participants might be long gone but the memories remain—and that's exactly how it should be.

Winston Churchill in pensive mood after the failure of the Dardanelles Campaign forced him out of office. Never one to shirk his duty, he resumed his career with the army and went to fight in France for a number of months.

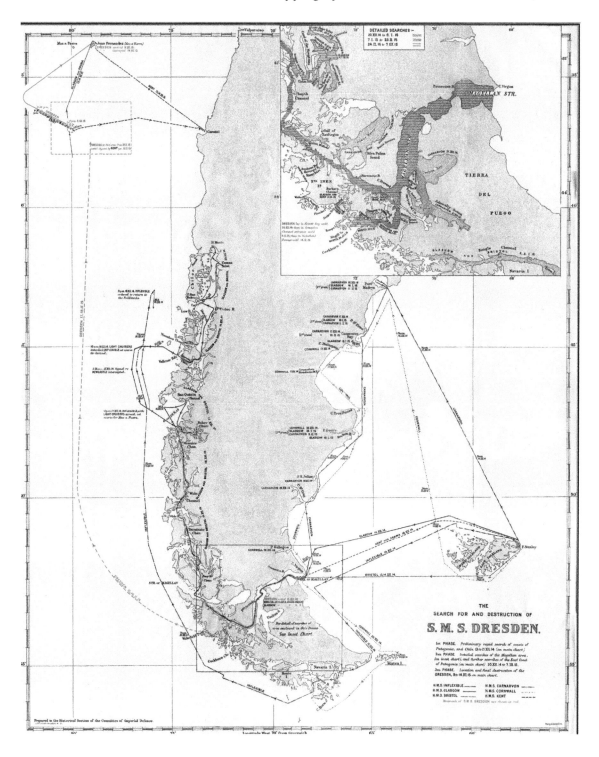

THE
SEARCH FOR AND DESTRUCTION OF
S. M. S. DRESDEN.

10

The Last Raider on the African Coast

When war broke out in August 1914 virtually all British troops were immediately removed from South Africa, leaving the invasion of German East Africa to be undertaken by local militia and by soldiers sent from India. It meant that, for the time being at least, German activity in the area and on the coast went on in a relatively untroubled manner.

The arrival in the region of the light cruiser *Königsberg*, under the command of Captain Max von Looff, did not worry the Admiralty overly much. She replaced the old gunboat Eber but despite being considerably faster and better armed, the powers that be in Whitehall still believed that Admiral King-Hall's Cape Squadron of antiquated cruisers would be strong enough to track her down and sink her.

King-Hall had to patrol and cover a 3,000 mile stretch of ocean but his situation was considerably boosted when Portugal put all her harbours and coal stocks on the East African coast at the disposal of the Allies. That left only Dar-es-Salaam in the German-held colony of Tanganyika for the *Königsberg* to take on coal. Even so, King-Hall's chance of encountering the German cruiser was slim unless Looff came out after one of the convoys taking troops from India to the Western Front.

King-Hall knew he had to do something to forestall the *Königsberg*. On 8 August the *Astraea* approached Dar-es-Salaam and began shelling the port and wireless station. When the Germans sank the port's floating dock in the harbour entrance, it might well have saved the town from further destruction but it also cut off the *Königsberg* from her base and its essential repair depot.

Captain Loof now had no option but to find sanctuary somewhere on the African coast, somewhere that the searching British would not find him. It was not an easy task and lesser men would have been daunted. Not Captain Looff.

The coast of Tanganyika was festooned with small channels and tiny harbours, many of them not shown on British maps of the time. In addition, the Germans had built a series of lookout stations along the coast, each of them with runners to carry information to places like Dar-es-Salaam. This, combined with an effective spy network in Zanzibar, meant that Captain Looff was almost always accurately informed about the strength of his enemies.

The Rufiji Delta

Having left Dar-es-Salaam before the *Astraea*'s bombardment, Captain Looff first headed for the Red Sea. He soon captured the *City of Winchester*, with its cargo of tea, and then coaled from the steamer *Somali*. He then sailed back across the Indian Ocean where, off the coast of Tanganyika, he again met with the *Somali*. Conditions on the open sea were not good for coaling, however, and it was clear that some better and more permanent arrangement would have to be made.

The skipper of the supply boat, who knew the area well, suggested the Rufiji Delta, an interwoven network of channels and creeks some 500 miles north of Dar-es-Salaam. It sounded reasonable and Looff was more than happy to see what the Delta had to offer.

A few days later the *Königsberg* was hidden in the Rufiji Delta at Salale. Lush vegetation and mangroves shielded her from watching eyes and, compared to that, the mosquitoes and crocodiles of the swamp counted for nothing. The enemy might search for months, Looff thought, and never come close to finding him.

Over the next few weeks the *Königsberg* was re-supplied by a succession of Arab dhows, paid for by the Governor of Tanganyika, that carried coal and food up the Delta. It was gruelling work for all concerned and it was clearly not the answer to the supply problem. But it was something and gradually Looff built up his provisions and coal stocks.

From the German information network, Looff now learned that the British and Continental press were confusing his ship with the other lone raider in the Indian Ocean, the *Emden*. The sense of panic amongst ship owners and merchant ship captains was almost tangible. Looff thought it hilariously funny but, more importantly, he saw that his ship was achieving the desired effect, even though she was still holed up in the Rufiji.

Sinking the Pegasus

Eventually, in the middle of September, Looff heard that a British cruiser had entered the port at Zanzibar. This was the aged *Pegasus* which had been constantly patrolling up and down the coast and had now, in desperate need of repair, come into harbour to clean her boilers.

Despite his orders to avoid confrontation with naval vessels and concentrate merely on commerce raiding, Looff was an adventurous and intelligent soul. He immediately decided on offensive action. At sunset on 19 September the *Königsberg* slipped her moorings and headed down the Channel towards the open sea. At dawn the following day Looff conned his ship past the tug *Helmuth*, acting as a guardship for the port, and made his way into Zanzibar. He was not challenged in any way—and that was the first mistake of the British forces. As the morning mist began to lift Looff silently but easily brought the *Königsberg* broadside on to the *Pegasus* and opened fire.

The British were taken totally by surprise and to begin with were unable to respond. Captain Inglis of the *Pegasus* did eventually manage to get his guns into play, after *Königsberg*'s third salvo, and did actually score some hits on the German ship, but by then it was too late. *Pegasus* was soon on fire and inside half an hour was a total wreck.[55]

Fearing other British ships might be in the area, Looff took one last shot at the WT station above the port—as it happened, the station was a dummy—and headed back out to sea. Behind him the shattered hull of the old *Pegasus* heeled over and sank. It had been a daring and adventurous attack on a British warship in what was, supposedly, a safe and well-guarded harbour and the German publicity machine was quick to trumpet the success.

The down side to the successful attack, of course, was that British prestige immediately demanded a response and the Admiralty, finally realising that the old cruisers of Admiral King-Hall really were inadequate for the task, a fleet of ships was hurriedly assembled to track down the *Königsberg*. These included the modern light cruisers *Chatham*, *Dartmouth* and *Weymouth*, all and any of them more than a match for the German ship. However, assembling the fleet was one thing, finding the quarry was another.

On the trip back to the Rufiji Delta the *Königsberg* began to develop serious engine trouble. She was clearly in need of a major overhaul—the very thing that, thanks to the blocking of Dar-es-Salaam, she could not get. Looff had received orders to head for South America where he would refuel, and then sail for Germany. Clearly, however, such a plan was now no longer possible.

Moored once more at Salale in the Rufiji Delta, Looff did the only thing he could do. He began to dismantle the ship's engines and send them overland by bullock cart and on the backs of African porters to the repair base at Dar-es-Salaam. In the rough outback where there were no roads or bridges, it threatened to be a long process.

The hull of the *Königsberg* was well camouflaged, trees and bushes being cut from the estuary banks and strapped to her funnels and masts. The crew came ashore to build observation posts and defensive strong points along the side of the Delta and its many channels, constructing a network of trenches that would not have seemed out of place on the plains of Flanders. Field guns were brought from Dar-es-Salaam while machine guns and other weapons from the *Königsberg* added to the strength of the defences.

Meanwhile the search for the raider continued. By the end of October the whole coast had been thoroughly examined—with the exception of the Rufiji Delta:–

It was thought unlikely that the German cruiser would be in hiding there because, as far as was known, the water was too shallow for a ship of *Königsberg*'s draught. At last a clue was obtained of her unexpected presence there through the capture of the steamer *President*, of the German East Africa Line, which had been working in secret with *Königsberg*.[56]

The old cruiser *Pegasus*, obsolete and no match for the guns of the raider *Königsberg*.

Running the Raider to Earth

Aided by charts taken from the *President*, at the end of October 1914 the cruiser *Chatham* moored off the Rufiji Delta. A landing party was sent ashore and natives confirmed that the *Königsberg* was moored further upstream. There were, they asserted, armed troops and sailors in the vicinity. When *Chatham* stood off the coast next morning the topmasts of two ships were spotted—the *Königsberg* and her faithful supply ship *Somali*.

The *Chatham* was soon joined by the *Dartmouth* and *Weymouth* and on 1 November they proceeded to sound the depth in the approach to the delta. They closed to within four and a half miles of the coast and *Chatham* was at last able to open fire on the *Somali*. As *Königsberg* was a mile and a half further inland she was still out of range.

Despite her lack of engines, the German cruiser moved slowly but steadily upstream, heading deeper and deeper into the swamps and jungle around the Rufiji. She used high tides and a process of warping in order to embed herself and certainly succeeded in keeping out of the range of British guns. All the time, soldiers from Dar-es-Salaam and sailors from the ship sat waiting in their positions along the banks to give her added protection.

Over the next few days the British ships crept closer inshore and by listing the ship five degrees to starboard, the *Chatham* was finally able to fire at the *Königsberg*. The bombardment continued for over half an hour, before the ebbing tide forced the *Chatham* to head out to sea again, but no significant damage was recorded.

It was clear that none of the British ships could reach the *Königsberg*, now some nine miles inland, and so it was decided to blockade her in the delta. The charts showed that the only channel by which the German vessel could leave was the Suninga, the narrowest part of which was close to the mouth. Despite heavy fire from German troops along the banks, the collier *Newbridge* was sailed up river and sunk across the exit. And there the matter rested, for the time being. Two of the British cruisers were recalled and with *Königsberg* entombed—still without her engine parts—the *Chatham* settled down to a lonely vigil, awaiting the spring tides.

The End of the Königsberg

It was July 1915 before the next attacks took place. At the beginning of the war three river monitors were in the process of being built in Britain for Brazil. These were immediately taken over by the Royal Navy and in 1915 two of them—the *Mersey* and *Severn*—were designated as the vessels to put an end to the menace of the *Königsberg*.

The monitors had very shallow draught, drawing just six feet. That made them poor sea boats but, with their six inch guns they were ideal ships to take on the Rufiji Delta. The voyage to the east coast of Africa took time and it was 3 June 1915 before the monitors were through the Suez Canal. When they arrived off the Rufiji, where they met with the Town Class cruisers of King-Hall's reinforced fleet, they were prepared for combat:–

> Plates and sandbag protection were erected on deck, and all the exposed parts of the ships, especially the propelling and steering gear, were guarded. Some 4000 kerosene tins, made waterproof, were stowed in all available compartments on each ship to provide buoyancy in case they were hulled below the waterline.[57]

Perhaps more significantly, a number of seaplanes now joined the operation. Co-operation between aircraft and ships was, at that time, still a revolutionary process and the use of modern technology like aeroplanes showed how serious the Admiralty considered the threat of the *Königsberg*. An aerodrome was created on nearby Mafia Island and reconnaissance flights made over the *Königsberg*, accurately plotting her position.

Finally, early on 5 July the two monitors weighed anchor and moved into the Rufiji Delta. They were supported by the *Weymouth* and the other light cruisers that took and returned fire from the German land batteries.

German field guns on the left bank of the Delta began firing as soon as the British ships were spotted. They were supported my maxim and rifle fire but, to begin with, little damage was done. The monitors sank a cutter and a gunboat and at 6.30 they moored close to an island in the middle of the stream, inland from the German batteries. Shortly afterwards they opened fire on the *Königsberg*, then some 10,000 yards away.

The *Königsberg* returned fire, aiming mainly at the *Mersey*. One shot destroyed the *Mersey*'s forward six inch turret and started a fire in the magazine hoist,

The cruiser *Chatham* which ran the *Königsberg* to earth in the Rufiji Delta and stayed to support the monitors in the final confrontation.

the blaze nearly causing an explosion that would have destroyed the ship. With shells falling close alongside she was forced to drop back by a thousand yards. The *Königsberg* promptly switched her attention to the *Severn*. The monitors were scoring hits, however, and soon one of the German's guns was out of action and a small fire started on board. Aided by observation from aircraft overhead, British firing continued all morning and into the afternoon. Then, at about 3.30, with little hope of a conclusion, the two monitors withdrew. As they passed downstream they kept up a withering fire against the German guns along the river bank. The open sea was reached just before 5.00 p.m. The British attack had been a serious attempt at destroying the *Königsberg*. But it had failed and the German defenders were jubilant. Looff, however, was realistic enough to know that the British would not stop here. The monitors would be back.

The Second Attempt

In the wake of the fruitless attack, aircraft observation reported that the *Königsberg* had been damaged but not seriously. She might yet escape. And so another attack was planned. On 18 July the two monitors were towed from their moorings at 8.00 a.m. and by midday were in position in the delta. Once again, aircraft were used to spot the fall of shot and to direct gunfire—one of them also dropped bombs on the German ship, ineffectually it must be said. British firing began shortly after midday and soon it was obvious that, aided

The monitor *Severn*, one of three river monitors being built for Brazil when the war broke out. Commandeered by the Royal Navy she, along with her sister ship *Mersey*, was shallow drafted enough to venture into the Delta.

HMS *Mersey*, the second of the river monitors to take part in the destruction of the *Königsberg*.

by reports and direction from the aircraft, the shells were striking home. Then the spotting aeroplane was hit by machine gun fire from the *Königsberg* and forced to land in the water, close to the *Mersey*. Despite somersaulting in an alarming fashion, both pilots escaped unhurt.

By now, however, the *Severn* had the range of the German cruiser and was pouring in shots at the rate of one a minute:–

> At 1.15 an explosion occurred on *Königsberg*, causing a bad fire which was never extinguished. She never fired a shot again after that. The second aeroplane now arrived, and *Mersey* proceeded to her prearranged station and opened fire on the enemy at 8200 yards. At this time *Königsberg*'s foremast was leaning heavily over. The top part of the mainmast had been shot away, and smoke was pouring out from its socket as it would from the mouth of a chimney, evidently coming from a fire below decks.[58]

The *Mersey* fired over twenty salvos at the badly damaged ship and soon the spotting aircraft reported that her central funnel had fallen. Then came the signal everyone was waiting for—'Target destroyed.'

In fact, the *Königsberg* did not sink immediately. But she had been grievously hurt and her hull slowly settled further and further into the Rufiji mud and silt. Captain Looff had been badly wounded in the battle but was still the last to leave the ship, setting the demolition charges that would finally end the career of this, the last German raider.

With the destruction of the *Königsberg* all German pretensions to power over the seas of the southern hemisphere finally vanished. It had taken five months for the British forces to destroy the main fleet of Admiral von Spee and hunt down the *Emden*, several months more to eliminate the menace of the last lone raiders, the *Dresden* and *Königsberg*. But once they were gone, British supremacy in the southern seas was assured. Trade could continue as normal. Britain was once more in command of the sea.

Conclusion

And so it was finally over, the campaign in the southern hemisphere, under twelve months from when it first began. There had been ups and downs, amazing highs and lows for both sides. However, when looked at from a distance, with the benefit of hindsight, it does seem as if there was little difference to the state of play between the situation in August 1914 and that existing once hostilities ended and the surviving ships returned to port.

Nearly four thousand men had died during the year. Nearly thirty merchant ships had been sunk as well as a dozen or so warships. But when all was said and done Britain had retained control of the southern seas and, it can be argued, the desperate battles of the previous twelve months simply need not have happened.

Perhaps that emphasizes the futility of war but it does not begin to explain why men so glibly and arrogantly take up arms at the merest whim of destiny. And, as if to reinforce the futility of it all, just twenty-five years later Britain and Germany once more came to blows in virtually the same seas. This time one of the combatants was named after the German admiral of 1914, the pocket battleship *Graff Spee* being a surface raider in the same ilk as the older *Scharnhorst* and *Gneisenau*.

There was no British ship named after Admiral Sturdee—that alone must say something about the British undervaluing their successful commanders—but two of the hunting cruisers were called after fabled Greek heroes so perhaps there was a sense of irony in that.

After the sinking of the *Königsberg* in the summer of 1915, war at sea began to take on a different tone. Kit Craddock and von Spee, along with the values and traditions they cherished, had clearly had their day—the world had moved on. Over the coming months and years, the advent of submarines, aircraft carriers and magnetic mines put an end to traditional naval warfare. It is still hard to work out if that is good or bad.

The sinking of the SMS *Königsberg*. For the first time, aircraft were used to direct the fire of ships onto the deck of the helpless cruiser.

Wreck of the SMS *Königsberg*, after the Battle of Rufiji Delta. The German cruiser was scuttled in the Rufiji Delta, Tanzania River, navigable for more than 100 km before emptying into the Indian Ocean about 200 km south of Dar es Salaam. (*Deutsches Bundesarchiv*)

The wrecked hull of the SMS *Königsberg* lies on the mud of the Rufiji Delta, no longer a threat to British shipping in the Indian Ocean.

Endnotes

1. *The South Wales Echo*, 15 July 1914.
2. *The South Wales Echo*, 3 August 1914.
3. German War Orders, 1914, quoted in Geoffrey Bennett *Coronel and Falklands*, p. 46.
4. *Ibid.*, p. 46.
5. Keith Middlemass *Command the Far Seas*, p. 90-91.
6. Admiralty telegram, 4 September 1914, quoted in Winston Churchill *The World Crisis*, p. 262.
7. Churchill, p. 207.
8. Telegram from Admiral Craddock to Admiralty, 8 October 1914, quoted in Churchill, p. 263.
9. Middelmass, p. 126.
10. WL Wyllie and MF Wren 'Sea Fights of the Great War,' p. 69.
11. *Ibid.*, p. 70-71.
12. Middlemass, p. 137.
13. Telegram from Admiral Craddock, 11 October 1914, quoted in Churchill, p. 264.
14. Telegram from Admiral Craddock, 18 October 1914, quoted in Churchill, p. 265.
15. Telegram from Admiral Craddock, 26 October 1914, quoted in Churchill, p. 269.
16. Churchill, p. 272.
17. Admiral von Spee, quoted in Middlemass, p. 168.
18. *Ibid.*, p. 170.
19. Letter from Lieutenant Otto von Spee, quoted in Wyllie and Wren, p. 92.
20. Richard Hough *The Pursuit of Admiral von Spee*, p. 116.
21. Churchill, p. 276-277.
22. Middlemass, p. 180.
23. Churchill, p. 279.
24. Bennett, p. 119.
25. Signal from Captain von Müller, quoted in Bennett, p. 63.

26. Hellmuth von Mücke, article quoted in Wyllie and Wren, p. 72.
27. *Ibid.*, p. 72.
28. *Ibid.*, p. 72.
29. *Ibid.*, p. 73.
30. *Ibid.*, p. 73.
31. *Ibid.*, p. 74.
32. Middlemass, p. 108.
33. Von Mucke, p. 75.
34. *Ibid.*, p. 76.
35. *Daily Telegraph*, November 1914.
36. Von Mücke, p. 77.
37. Middlemass, p. 112.
38. Julian Thompson *The War at Sea, 1914–1918*, p. 113.
39. Churchill, p. 285.
40. Wyllie and Wren, p. 100.
41. Anon, article published in *The Manchester Guardian History of the War*, p. 40.
42. *Ibid.*, p. 40.
43. *Ibid.*, p. 40.
44. *Ibid.*, p. 40.
45. *Ibid.*, p. 40.
46. *Ibid.*, p. 41.
47. Anon, article published in Wyllie and Wren, p. 111.
48. *Ibid.*, p. 110.
49. Churchill, p. 287.
50. Wyllie and Wren, p. 44.
51. *Ibid.*, p. 49.
52. Article, quoted in Wyllie and Wren, p. 49.
53. Middlemass, p. 228.
54. Phil Carradice *The Great War*, p. 72.
55. Middlemass, p. 81.
56. Wyllie and Wren, p. 116.
57. *Ibid.*, p. 120.
58. *Ibid.*, p. 123.

Bibliography

Primary Sources

The South Wales Echo, July to December 1914.
The Daily Telegraph, November 1914.
The Manchester Guardian, 1914 to 1915.
The Manchester Guardian History of the War, 1914–1915, Vol. 2.
The Western Mail, August to December 1914.
Diary of Captain J. D. Allen

Secondary Sources

Geoffrey Bennett, *Coronel and Falklands*, (Pan Books, London, 1967).
Phil Carradice, *The Great War*, (Amberley, Stroud, 2010).
Winston Churchill, *The World Crisis, 1911 to 1918*, (Four Square, London, undated).
Richard Hough, *The Pursuit of Admiral von Spee*, (Periscope Publishing, London, 2003).
H. M. Le Fleming, *Warships of World War One*, (Ian Allan, London, undated).
Keith Middlemass, *Command the Far Seas*, (Hutchinson, London, 1961).
Jan Morris, *Fisher's Face*, (Penguin, London, 1996).
A. B. Sainsbury and F. L. Phillips, *The Royal Navy Day by Day*, (Sutton, Stroud, 2005).
A. J. P. Taylor, *The First World War*, (Penguin, London, 1963).
Julian Thompson, *The War at Sea, 1914–1918*, (Imperial War Museum/Pan, London, 2006).
Wilfred Pym Trotter, *The Royal Navy in Old Photographs*, (J. M. Dent, London, 1975).
W. L. Wyllie and M. F. Wren, *Sea Fights of the Great War*, (Cassell and Co., London, 1918).

Index